Drug-Taking Behavior
Among School-Aged Youth:
The Alaska Experience
and Comparisons
with Lower-48 States

Drug-Taking Behavior Among School-Aged Youth: The Alaska Experience and Comparisons with Lower-48 States

Bernard Segal, PhD

Routledge
Taylor & Francis Group

NEW YORK AND LONDON

Drug-Taking Behavior Among School-Aged Youth: The Alaska Experience and Comparisons with Lower-48 States has also been published as *Drugs & Society*, Volume 4, Numbers 1/2 1989.

First published 1990 by The Haworth Press, Inc.

2 Park Square, Milton Park, Abingdon, Oxfordshire OX14 4RN
52 Vanderbilt Avenue, New York, NY 10017

Routledge is an imprint of the Taylor & Francis Group, an informa business

First issued in paperback 2019

Library of Congress Cataloging-in-Publication Data

Segal, Bernard.
 Drug-taking behavior among school-aged youth : the Alaska experience and comparisons with lower-48 states / Bernard Segal.
  p. cm.
 "Has also been published as Drugs & society, volume 4, numbers 1/2, 1989" — T.p. verso.
 Includes bibliographical references.
 ISBN 0-86656-966-9
 1. Teenagers — Alaska — Drug use. 2. Teenagers — United States — States — Drug use.
3. Drug abuse surveys — Alaska. 4. Drug abuse surveys — United States — States. I. Title.
HV5824.Y68S44   1990
362.29'12'0835 — dc20   89-29119
                                                                                                  CIP

ISBN 13: 978-0-86656-966-8 (hbk)
ISBN 13: 978-1-138-87311-7 (pbk)

MIX
Paper from
responsible sources
FSC   FSC™ C013985
www.fsc.org

Printed in the United Kingdom
by Henry Ling Limited

Drug-Taking Behavior Among School-Aged Youth: The Alaska Experience and Comparisons with Lower-48 States

CONTENTS

ABOUT THE AUTHOR

Bernard Segal, PhD, is Associate Dean of the School of Health Sciences at the University of Alaska Anchorage. Dr. Segal began at the University of Alaska in 1977 as Training Coordinator within the Center for Alcohol and Addiction Studies. He was named the Center's Director in 1979 and continued in that role until June 1983, when he returned to full time research and teaching. He was reappointed as the Center's Director in August 1987, and appointed to his current position in April 1988.

His research interest is in the psychosocial correlates of drug-taking behavior. A recipient of both federal and state grants, his research has led to two books, numerous publications and presentations, and to collaboration with researchers in other countries. He has been to Israel and Japan as a visiting professor, and has been invited to the Soviet Union, where he is currently involved in a collaborative project with alcohol researchers in Novosibirisk, Siberia.

After earning a doctorate in clinical psychology from the University of Oklahoma in 1967, Dr. Segal taught at the University of Rhode Island for several years before becoming Director of the Psychological Center and of Clinical Training at Murray State University in Kentucky. During this time, he was also a police psychologist at the Murray Police Department.

Dr. Segal is the editor of *Drugs & Society*.

Preface

Research findings are an important, but often overlooked element in helping to shape program and policy planning. The current research, conducted during 1977 and 1988, and funded in large part by a grant from the Alaska State Office of Alcoholism and Drug Abuse, Department of Health and Social Services, is the second study of drug-taking behavior among Alaskan youth in grades 7-12. It was designed to provide local and state policy makers and planners with information to aid in developing initiatives for addressing smoking, drinking, and drug use among early adolescents and teenagers.

Knowledge of the extent, or prevalence of drug use, is basic to planning strategies to prevent or reduce drug-taking behavior among youth. Prevalence, as used here, represents an estimate of the number or proportion of students who reported having had experience with one or more illicit chemical substances, alcohol, or tobacco, in the form of cigarettes or smokeless or chewing tobacco. In the sections to follow, the findings are presented on demographic variations on the prevalence of drug-taking behavior related to basic planning units — grade, gender, ethnicity, and regions.

This report furnishes information on both the extent and patterns of drug, alcohol, and tobacco use among Alaskan youth. This document primarily concentrates on describing demographic variations in the extent of drug, alcohol, and tobacco use among students in grades 7-12, and compares the major findings with those reported from an earlier survey of the same grade levels conducted during 1981 and 1982. Of specific importance, however, are comparisons with findings from other states and with national studies. Since Alaska was not included in any national studies, and because prevalence levels in Alaska have been shown to be higher than reported in national samples (Segal, 1983a, 1983b), these comparisons provide an important data base from which to review national findings and to gauge the patterns of drug-taking behavior among school-age youth. It is anticipated that the information gained from this report can be used to help further a general understanding of drug-taking behavior, and assist those involved in efforts to reduce and prevent drug-taking behavior among youth.

Bernard Segal, PhD

Acknowledgments

There are many people to thank for their generous assistance. Ellen R. Segal, my research assistant, was responsible for coding each questionnaire, entering the data in the computer, and establishing the data base. She worked diligently and responsibly, overseeing that each questionnaire was accurate and that the data were entered correctly. Her conscientiousness insured that the data were both reliable and valid.

My colleague, Dennis G. Fisher, Ph.D., provided invaluable assistance. His willingness to share ideas, review and edit drafts, and offer critical analysis, was of significant help to me as I strove to interpret the data. Thank you Dennis!

Marguerite Lambert provided important technical assistance, editing, and typing when necessary. Her assistance is deeply appreciated.

As usual, the staff of the University of Alaska Anchorage's Office of Computing & Technology was there when I needed help. Ron Langly, its Director, always cheerful, saw that I was never left without technical assistance. I am especially appreciative of the help provided by Victor Kapella, who found solutions to problems that seemed insurmountable to me. It has been a pleasure to observe Victor grow and mature as a professional program analyst. The "nodies" were also always available and helpful. Pam Woods, Valerie L. Johnston, and Tamara L. Case, among others, deserve special thanks.

This research could not have been accomplished without the assistance of the many school officials in the participating districts. Too numerous to name here, I would nevertheless like to thank all of them for their help. I would also like to thank the students who volunteered to participate in the study. This research would not have been possible without their trust. Finally, I would like to extend my appreciation to the Coordinator of the State Office of Alcoholism and Drug Abuse, Mat Felix, and to his staff, for their valuable assistance.

Chapter 1

Introduction

The problem of drug use[1] within the United States has emerged as one of the more highly publicized yet least understood phenomena among contemporary health and social problems. This state of affairs is directly related to the rapid and dramatic increase in drug use, particularly among youth, over the past twenty to thirty years. The problem of drug use developed so rapidly that it initially precluded any concentrated attempts to develop an understanding of *how* and *why* drugs became incorporated so quickly into the national lifestyle. During the early 1960s research efforts consisted largely of studies that tried to identify psychosocial correlates of drug use (Segal, 1988). Few studies tried to gain data about the nature and extent of drug use. Instead, efforts were mainly directed at determining the extent to which drug users, primarily college-age students, were deviant—both psychologically and socially (Anglin, Thompson, & Fisher, 1986; Segal, Huba, & Singer, 1980). Many of these studies, however, often yielded contradictory and piecemeal findings and, for the most part, did not provide adequate information to help direct proper and relevant countermeasures (Segal, 1988). It was not until the late 1960s that efforts began to shift away from research which reacted to the problem to research that tried to gain a perspective on the problem.

In 1966 the National Institute on Drug Abuse (NIDA), in order to begin to achieve a perspective on the prevalence of drug use within the United States, sponsored a large nationwide study to begin to acquire information about the nature and extent of drug use among the nation's high school seniors (Johnston, 1973). This project has

---

1. Since illicit drug use constitutes the problem to be addressed within this research, the terms "drug abuse," "drug use," and "drug-taking behavior" will be used interchangeably in the text of this document.

since evolved into an ongoing study, of which the latest findings were released by NIDA in February, 1989 (NIDA, 1989). In 1977, NIDA commissioned the first national household survey designed to monitor the extent of illicit drug use in the nation among youth (ages 12-17), young adults (ages 18-25), and adults (ages 26 +) (Cisin, Miller & Harrell, 1978). The national survey has since been maintained, with the latest findings having recently been released which described the pattern and prevalence of drug use in the nation during 1988 (NIDA, 1989). These studies, together with other survey research funded by NIDA (summarized in Richards, 1981), have helped to provide a clearer perspective on the nature and extent of drug use in the United States.

DRUG USE IN ALASKA

Alaska, however, was not included in any national study. Because information about the nature and extent of drug use within Alaska was lacking, there was no data base or framework to measures changes in patterns and prevalence of drug use over given time periods. Nor was there a basis for comparing levels of drug use within the state to prevalence statistics reported for the 48 contiguous states ("lower-48" states). The need for a broad-based epidemiological study in Alaska was imperative because Alaska, with its mainly youthful population and its "last frontier" atmosphere, was alleged to have a high prevalence of drug use.

The need to gain information about drug use in the state was realized by the State Office of Alcohol and Drug Abuse (SOADA) when, in 1981, it commissioned a study by the Center for Alcohol and Addiction Studies (CAAS), University of Alaska Anchorage, to ascertain the nature and pattern of drug-taking behavior in the state (Segal, 1983a, 1983b). This study consisted of two parts: (1) a survey of the general population 18 years and older (Community Study), and (2) a survey of youth in grades 7-12 (School Study). The latter research involved studying eight widely-separated urban and rural school districts representative of the different regions of Alaska, except for the Aleutian chain. The locations were Anchorage, Barrow, Bethel, Fairbanks, Juneau, Kotzebue, Nome, and Sitka. These sites were picked to obtain a representative sample of the state's junior and senior high school students. The Community Study, except for Nome, was conducted in the same sites.

The results of both studies were reported in 1983 (Segal, 1983a, 1983b). Briefly, the findings show that lifetime use of a drug (ever tried) is higher among school age youth between 12 to 17 years, and adults 18 and older, than among comparable groups found in the lower-48 states. These findings confirm higher levels of drug use in Alaska than in the lower-48 states.

THE SCHOOL FOLLOW-UP STUDY

The present research, also under the auspices of SOADA, is a follow-up study of the initial school study undertaken during 1981-1982 (Segal, 1983a). There were two primary reasons to resurvey school age youth: (1) the need to determine how the pattern and extent of drug use had changed over time among youth, and (2) to attempt to determine what effects prevention efforts, introduced in the interval between the initial and follow-up surveys, may have had. The study's specific objectives are:

1. To obtain demographic information about adolescents in grades 7-12 in relation to use or nonuse of chemical substances.
2. To obtain information on the prevalence of specific chemical substances, including alcohol and tobacco.
3. To obtain data about patterns of drug-taking behavior, including alcoholic beverages and tobacco products.
4. To obtain information about some of the consequences of drug-taking behavior.
5. To compare Alaska's findings with comparable data from other states and with national studies.

The findings should have important implications for planning and policy development by governmental authorities, both in and outside of Alaska, in their efforts to understand and deal with the health, social, economic, and legal consequences of drug-taking behavior.

Chapter 2

A Historical Review of Drug Use in Alaska

DRUGS AND THE OIL PIPELINE
CONSTRUCTION PERIOD (1974-1978)

As early as 1973, in planning for the potential effect of drug use expected from the construction of the oil pipeline to start in 1974, the State of Alaska recognized that it was confronting a "potential nonnormal crisis situation, and will have to adopt unusual methods to cope with this unusual situation" (Poppe, 1973, p. 1). Before this time drug use was not considered by health authorities to be a significant problem in the state. Except for marijuana use, and a few heroin addicts, the state considered itself to be isolated from the large-scale drug problems that were being experienced in the lower-48 states because of Alaska's physical separation from the rest of the country.

By the early 1970s, however, research was beginning to show that the drug-taking behavior which had permeated school-age youth in the lower-48 states had started to manifest itself in Alaska. Porter and her associates (1973), for example, found that 36.6 percent of Anchorage's school children (grades 6-12) had used one or more drugs other than alcohol or tobacco at least once, and that 19.8 percent had used drugs during the past seven days before being surveyed; 4.5 percent had also reported using drugs four or more times in the last seven days. Marijuana was the most commonly used drug, followed by solvents, stimulants, amphetamines, hashish, mescaline, and peyote. It was noted in the study that multiple drug use was evident, and that the prevalence of reported drug use exceeded such reports for students in Dallas, Texas, and in San Mateo, California (Porter et al., 1973).

The importance of these findings was apparently overlooked in the state's efforts to prepare for the health, social, and economic impacts of the pipeline construction. Had they been used they could have indicated that there was an immediate need to address drug use, at least among youth. Such efforts might have helped to minimize the adverse effects of substance abuse on youth during the pipeline construction era.

Although it was recognized that alcohol and drug use would increase after the pipeline construction started, the state did not take any specific steps to prepare itself for the projected increase, and was unprepared for the dramatic changes it was to undergo concerning drug and alcohol use. After the pipeline was proceeding, the state tended to focus its resources on the problems resulting from a significant increase in alcohol consumption, and only limited attempts were made to assess or to begin to deal with other forms of drug use. The state was especially hampered in its effort to respond to the drug problem because there was little information available about drug use in the state to enable health planners to anticipate needs.

The then State Office of Drug Abuse, which was the official agency charged with the responsibility for compiling statistics, and with developing treatment and prevention strategies, could only estimate drug use in Alaska in the mid 1970s. It reported as follows:

> In Alaska, the major drug abuse problem is multiple drug use — that is, the use of a combination of drugs which may also include alcohol. This problem is the most severe both in terms of numbers of users, and in the potential for causing physical damage.
>
> It is difficult to describe the drug-abusing population in Alaska. Clearly, young people are involved, and they come most frequently in arrest and treatment statistics. Young adults and middle-aged individuals (particularly women) also impact the treatment and social service system, but their numbers are not known.

Native substance abuse rates appear to be higher than non-native rates, but this may be partly a reflection of greater Native use of public social service agencies as opposed to private physicians.

The major substances abused after multiple abuse are tranquilizers and anti-depressants, primarily among urban, non-native females age 36-50; and narcotic analgesics, including heroin and codeine. Prescription medications made up a large number of the cases in this category.

The precise nature and extent of the drug abuse problem is unclear at this time. It is expected that . . . the coming year [will] give . . . [a] more accurate picture. (State Office of Drug Abuse, 1975, pp. 1-3)

By this time, the state had begun to experience the first effect of the oil pipeline construction project, and the information it needed to deal with drug use was late in coming. Additionally, what information that was available was considered to be incomplete because it was derived from a limited population, and because "the rapidity of social and economic change in the state invite caution in interpreting the . . . statistics" (State Office of Drug Abuse, 1976, p. 21). More important, however, inadequate information meant that there was no way of precisely determining to what extent the incidence and prevalence of drug use in the state was affected by the construction of the pipeline.[1]

That the construction of the transalaska pipeline (1974 to 1978) affected drug use in the state is undisputable. This effect is well illustrated in a report by the Alaska State Troopers in 1976, which described the problem of drug use as "growing to such magnitude that illicit drugs were coming into Alaska by every conceivable means imaginable, and the drugs were being distributed to virtually

---

1. It should be noted that the lack of information about who impacts the treatment and social service system, with specific respect to alcohol and drug-related problems, has since been rectified. A statewide management information system (MIS), developed by the State Office of Alcoholism and Drug Abuse (SOADA), became operational in 1983, and important data about client utilization of alcohol and drug treatment programs has since been reported by SOADA.

every city and village in Alaska" (Department of Public Safety, 1976, p. 2).

Because reliable data were lacking to serve as a baseline to gauge what changes happened, this lack obstructed any attempts to identify related impacts that may have occurred in the state. It is therefore difficult to accurately determine the extent to which the pipeline contributed to the increase in drug use, and to identify the adverse health, social, and economic impacts related to drug use. Only general estimates or qualitative accounts of events are possible.

Lonner (1983), in a comprehensive review of the health and social impacts of substance abuse during the pipeline construction period, described the few years of the pipeline construction as follows:

> [It] . . . resulted in a new population entering Alaska which, because of its work force character (younger 20-29 and older 44-59, single, male, skilled and unskilled), exaggerated (through massive over-representation of these characteristics) the already skewed character of the resident Alaska population. Placing this new population atop the existing population, given some level of interaction between them, and compounding this situation with the excitement, wages, and other features of the project resulted in very expectable outcomes. (p. VII-8)

One of the outcomes of this situation was a rise in substance use in the state, especially marijuana and cocaine. Lonner (1983) indicated that the use of cocaine and marijuana was probably directly related to the prevalence of money, and to the earlier derived (drug) habits pipeline workers brought with them to Alaska. A general assessment of the changes related to the construction of the Alaska Pipeline was outlined by Lonner:

1. An increase in marijuana use among the young.
2. An increase in concurrent poly-drug use (e.g., alcohol, marijuana and cocaine) resulting in a number of disabilities.
3. A lowering of the age for beginning drug use.

4. An increase in petty crimes related to obtaining money for drugs.
5. A continuing or increased tolerance for alcohol as a substance of choice for young people, particularly when abandoning or diminishing use of other substances and emulating the behaviors of their parents.
6. A continuing disapprobation of drugs by parents but more tolerance of youthful drinkers.
7. Continued excessive use of licit drugs.
8. Increasing penetration of all age groups of cocaine, based on ability to pay.

Attempts by the State Office of Drug Abuse to estimate drug use, beginning in 1976, were first made by evaluating information about clients who entered treatment programs funded by state agencies. Although it is difficult to generalize from such data, it nevertheless provided some basis for describing drug use. These data show that out of 491 clients who entered a drug treatment program between July 1974 and June 1975, the largest number were admitted for a heroin related problem (31%). Problems with marijuana were second (12%), followed by amphetamines (10%), hallucinogens (4%), barbiturates (3%), and cocaine (2%). The report concluded that "drug abuse problems in Alaska appear to be increasing . . . and [are] reflected in a dramatic increase in heroin addicts entering treatment" (State Office of Drug Abuse, 1976, p. 27). As a result of these findings the State office of Drug Abuse focused its efforts on addressing this addiction problem, investing both money and resources to support established narcotic drug treatment programs and to start new ones.

The State Office of Drug Abuse also recognized that it lacked hard data on drug use in the state, particularly about the effects of the pipeline on drug-taking behavior. Instead of such data the State Office provided qualitative information in the form of anecdotal reports from communities directly impacted by the pipeline construction. The report tried to identify the treatment, rehabilitation and prevention needs that were perceived as necessary to combat substance abuse.

The description of the problems faced by the Municipality of

Anchorage is an excellent characterization of the problems that the state as a whole was experiencing (State Office of Drug Abuse, 1976):

> Youth in the City of Anchorage, who constitute almost 40% of the population, are raised in a boomtown atmosphere that fosters immense cultural and communal dislocations. Anchorage as the center of the population in the state of Alaska and major transportation network for the entire state, has experienced an accelerated growth in population due to the discovery of oil on the Northern Slope and concomitant pipeline construction activities. It is a city that is rapidly being transformed from the community it was a few short years ago to a rapidly growing metropolitan area with all the inherent problems of such growth.
>
> Population growth in the Anchorage area increased by six percent between the first two quarters of 1975 and last two quarters of the same year. Most of that growth is largely due to immigration of a highly transient population seeking the wealth they had dreamed of in the "lower forty-eight." Many are single, unattached pipeline construction workers, who at peak season work nine-week shifts on the pipeline. Many return to Anchorage for a two-week rest and recuperation with more money in their pockets than they'd ever dreamed of earning. At this time they begin venting their frustrations in any way available.
>
> Many of these new immigrants as well as Alaskans must live separate from their families during these nine-week periods. Housewives are often left alone with small children in desperate isolation during the long and dark winter months without the familiar support of family and friends. The additional stresses imposed by this life-style are destructive to one degree or another on all but the most solid relationships between people. The price being paid for the boom is reflected in such social indicators as the increasing divorce rate in Anchorage; the rapidly increasing reports of child abuse and neglect;

and reports of increasing school vandalism in the city to the extent that armed security guards are being permanently stationed in city schools.

Many newcomers to the area were strong, independent people seeking increased opportunities. At the same time many new arrivals can only be considered "misfits" who desperately see Alaska as their last chance for life improvements. Many of these people have brought with them a life-style of misery which is further intensified by the apparent abundance of others surrounding them. One measure of the depth of frustration and powerlessness felt by these people are indications of increasing drug use.

The severity of the problem is increasing and is reflected by the increase of heroin among youth. As the incidence, as well as the social and economic costs of drug abuse steadily rises, the need for resources to combat drug abuse problems becomes imperative. (Lonner, 1983, pp. 10-14)

When the state organized its efforts to fully combat the problem of drug abuse, the pipeline construction period was over, and some effects were immediately noticeable. Lonner (1983) indicated that following the pipeline period, which ended in late 1978, a variety of changes were noted about substance abuse:

1. A decline in the range of available drugs, particularly amphetamines, tranquilizers, and LSD.
2. A decline in the prevalence of cocaine due to money non-availability.
3. A stabilization of marijuana use, particularly in the 18-30 year old group.
4. A lowering in the age of drug experimentation.
5. Increasing resemblance between parents' and children's substance-of-choice, particularly alcohol and marijuana, as children mature.

6. A greater variation and differentiation of habits and fads among younger populations (health fads, religions, etc.). (p. VIII-38)

POST-PIPELINE PERIOD (1979-1989)

The full effect that the pipeline construction era had on the state, and on the health, economic and social consequences of substance use and abuse, was not fully realized until 1979. At that time the newly formed State Office of Alcoholism and Drug Abuse (SOADA), which was created by the legislature in 1977 to coordinate the state's efforts to combat substance abuse, began to compile data that allowed it to assess the nature and extent of drug use in Alaska. SOADA's aim was to not only try to use this information to identify populations at risk of becoming abusers, but also to use it to begin to develop treatment and prevention strategies. Also, SOADA began to formulate new data gathering procedures that would help to make a conclusive analysis of drug use in the state possible.

The initial results of SOADA's analysis were reported in its *Drug Abuse Plan for 1979* (SOADA, 1979), which represents the first effort to assess comprehensively the nature and extent of drug use in the state, and to characterize some health, social and economic consequences that substance abuse had in Alaska. What is revealed is that a substantial change in drug-taking behavior and its effects had occurred. On the one hand the incidence and prevalence of drug use rose greatly after the start of the construction of the pipeline, and the adverse affects of such use, such as drug-related arrests, deaths, accidents, treatment admissions, etc., rose accordingly. On the other hand, after the pipeline, these figures show declines, but remain at a level higher than before the impact of the pipeline.

There was little doubt that the pipeline construction period left a substantial legacy, both positive and negative, on the state. With respect to substance abuse, it appears not only to have reinforced those drug-taking behaviors that had been established, but to have also introduced new patterns of use, and to have spread such behavior to all segments of Alaskan society, particularly to the younger members of Alaska's population.

HEALTH, SOCIAL, AND ECONOMIC IMPACTS RELATED TO DRUG USE

Until recently estimates of drug use in Alaska were not obtained from samples of the general population. Instead, the State office of Alcoholism and Drug Abuse (SOADA), which was responsible for tabulating data on drug use, relied on getting data from indirect indices, that is, characterizing and analyzing data that were believed "to relate to drug use in such a way that changes in the indicators correspond to change in actual drug abuse patterns" (SOADA, 1979, p. 1). It was assumed if several indicators were analyzed together, and if consistent patterns were observed, over time, then these indirect indicators could have provided a reliable indication of the nature and extent of drug abuse within the state. While such a procedure may provide data indicative of a special population of drug abusers, the use of such data to reflect on prevalence of drug use among the general population is very restricted. But even if such data cannot be used to generalize to the population as a whole, the data nevertheless provide information pertinent to a needs assessment, and yields information relevant to the full scope of prevention and treatment activities.

The State Office of Alcohol and Drug Abuse picked a variety of indicators to estimate drug abuse in the state. Some indices were: drug-related mortality data, drug treatment program admission statistics, mental health data, and criminal justice data.

Drug Treatment Program Data: 1982-1983

The initiation of a new management information system by SOADA in 1982 enabled the State Office to accurately assess all client admissions to state funded programs. Between October 1, 1982 and September 30, 1983, 13,400 admissions were reported by the 35 alcohol and drug programs funded by state monies. Of these, 9,681 were unduplicated admissions. Evaluation of these data reveal that out of a subgroup of 12,711 cases, 6.44 percent are for drug-related problems. (Alcohol-related problems accounted for the remaining number of cases.)

Surprisingly, drug-related admissions accounted for a small percentage of cases in proportion to alcohol-related admissions, and of those drug-related cases that came to the attention of treatment programs, problems with marijuana and cocaine represented the largest number of cases.

Criminal Justice Data

Although criminal justice data are available, it should be noted that problems exist with using such data. Because Alaska's drug laws and enforcement policies have changed over the past few years it is difficult to determine how criminal justice data should be interpreted. Are increases or decreases in statistics, for example, attributable to changes in the laws or to greater emphasis on law enforcement? There is little doubt that an interaction effect is at work, but it is extremely difficult to parcel out the extent that each factor has contributed to any changes in criminal justice statistics. Nevertheless, such data afford an opportunity to monitor trends in drug use and to gain information (e.g., age, race, gender, etc.,) about who has been arrested or detained for drug-related offenses.

A review of arrest statistics for drug-related offenses from 1973 to 1977 gives evidence that marijuana-related arrests account for the highest proportion, averaging about 60 percent of all drug arrests. Cocaine-related arrests range from 5.5 to 17.4 percent, averaging 9.9 percent over this period. Arrests for heroin-related charges average 5.7 percent of all drug arrests. Arrests for possession or sale of stimulants amount to 7.6 percent of all drug arrests. The trend over this time span (1973-1977) was for a high percentage of juvenile arrests, that is, for persons 19 years of age and under, for marijuana-related charges. Most persons arrested for narcotics violations were in the 20-29 age group. The clear majority of arrests involved Caucasians.

More recent data for 1981-1982 show an increase in narcotic-related arrests. Between 1977-79, narcotics arrests account for 11.6 percent of all drug arrests, while in 1981-82 this category increased to 25 percent of all drug arrests. Between 1980-1981 those 18 and under constituted most arrests (55% in 1980; 57.5% in 1981), and men outnumber women by better than a 5:1 ratio.

Statistics reported by the Alaska State Troopers (Department of Public Safety, 1988) for the period January 1, 1986 through June

30, 1987, show that a total of 521 drug-related arrests were made, and that street drug seizures amounted to over $12 million.

The criminal justice system, however, had concerns that transcended the problem of having to deal with only alcohol and drug users or traffickers. An analysis of sex offenders (Analysis, 1985), for example, shows that of the 350 sex offenders incarcerated in Alaska starting March 1, 1989, 31 percent of the cases needed some form of treatment intervention for alcohol or drug abuse at the time of sentencing.

Based on these data it may be concluded that drug use exists in Alaska. Although most of this use can be directly related to the pipeline construction period, the major drug-related effects from this period seem to have bottomed out. The state has entered a new period where current drug use, although rooted in the pipeline years, has become more closely related to contemporary events. As such, drug-taking behavior needs to be understood not only in terms of its antecedent causes, but also in terms of its current correlates and effects; this information needs to be obtained for the population as a whole, and not only from specific segments of the population.

As noted above, most of the information about drug use in Alaska has been largely found from indirect indices or secondary sources that reflect drug use among special populations, thereby significantly limiting efforts to arrive at inferences about the nature and extent of drug-taking behaviors that happen in the general population. Stated differently, despite all the information that was compiled, there was no definitive data on who in the general population was involved in drug use, and the nature and extent of such use. The need for such information was clearly recognized by Alaska's State Office of Alcoholism and Drug Abuse which, in 1981, undertook an effort to fill this void through a research grant awarded to the Center for Alcohol and Addiction Studies (CAAS), at the University of Alaska Anchorage (Segal, 1983a, 1983b). The purpose of that study was to assess the extent and pattern of substance use in relation to demographic, social and psychological factors, as well as to identify the frequency, context and consequences of drug use among school-age youth (School Study) in grades 7-12, and members of the general population 18 and older (Community Study). The findings were evaluated in terms of the unique characteristics of Alaska's environment, as well as in terms of the influences that the pipeline construction had on the state.

The results of the 1983 school study are reported in Chapter 5, where they are compared with the findings from the current study.

The findings from the community study have been reported elsewhere (Segal, 1983b). Some of the major findings are summarized below:

- The overall level of lifetime prevalence (tried a drug one or more times) was high, with 57.3% of those sampled having indicated that they had tried at least one chemical substance, excluding alcohol.
- Of the drugs used, the three most prevalent were marijuana, stimulants and cocaine.
- Comparison by age groups showed that drug use was more prevalent in the 18-25 age group than in the 26+ group.
- Prevalence rates in Alaska for both the 18-25 and 26+ age groups exceeded prevalence rates for comparable groups in the lower-48 states.

MARIJUANA, SOCIAL VALUES, AND LEGISLATION IN ALASKA

One of the more interesting aspects about Alaska is that when the events that occurred during the past 10-15 years are examined, it can be surmised that Alaska represents a contemporary microcosm of development that other western states went through as they developed from territories into states, especially when their economies were stimulated by rapid population growth and resource development. As a consequence of its recent boom economy Alaska attracted a flock of migrants, many coming to seek new starts, away from troubles and problems that haunted them in their previous locales. Others come because they were lured by the promise of high paying jobs (only to find out that these were generally unavailable). Nevertheless, many of these persons shared a desire to be part of the "last frontier." Because of this last frontier ethic, Alaska tended to attract people who advocated a strong antipathy to conformity and for laws that are perceived as infringing on individual freedoms.

For many of these people, laws regulating drugs are interpreted as arbitrary and there is a tendency to disregard them, especially when marijuana is involved. Yet there is also a core of long-time Alaskans and some newer migrant families who tend to represent more traditional values, attitudes that are in sharp contrast to those held by many recent arrivals. Efforts to deal with marijuana use in the state have thus been met with strong resistance by some groups while intensely advocated by others.

These differences are readily apparent by the public's response to legislative attempts to strengthen drug laws pertaining to marijuana. As a result of a ruling by the state's Supreme Court (Ravin *v.* State of Alaska, 1975) that adults could possess marijuana for personal use within their own homes based on the rights to privacy section in Alaska's Constitution, the legislature, shortly after this decision, decriminalized personal use of marijuana. Alaskans were thus able to possess a small amount of marijuana within their *own* homes for personal use, but could not transport or sell it. Alaska's recently revised criminal code (enacted in 1982), in conformance with earlier legislation, allows up to but not including four (4) ounces of marijuana for personal possession under well-defined conditions.

Following the changes in the State Code, which liberalized the amount of marijuana that one could possess in the privacy of one's home, the Alaska State Legislature has repeatedly attempted to reinstate criminal penalties for possession of marijuana. One of the more serious attempts was initiated in 1984, but it failed largely because of a lack of widespread support. The testimony given at public hearings reflected the controversy and conflicting attitudes about marijuana in the state. On one side people protested that any new laws would make people vulnerable to police action in that the police could bust a "pot party" inside a private home. One person testified that the new law would create "a body of criminals out of law-abiding citizens whose only crime is to smoke marijuana in their own homes" (Barrett, 1984).

An opposing view on decriminalization was expressed in a Letter to the Editor in one of Anchorage's newspapers soon after the above testimony was reported. The author of this letter wrote because of his belief that:

the crude drug marijuana is an extremely destructive and dangerous substance. Once a person is under its influence their own reasoning becomes subservient to the mind-altering chemicals that it contains. The false sense of pleasure that can accompany this chemical "high" can seduce the brain and result in a psychological dependence and a loss of the ability to experience natural pleasure. . . . Marijuana should no longer be legally available in this state and . . . legislation aimed at ending our liberal laws . . . [should be supported]. (Konet, 1984, p. 12)

The arguments for and against recriminalization of marijuana have continued, with no legislative acts having been enacted to date to change the existing law. One of the more serious attempts at corrective legislation arose during the 1988 legislative session. At that time a bill was introduced in the Alaska State Senate (Senate Bill 32 — "An act relating to marijuana; and providing for an effective date") to essentially recriminalize possession of marijuana. The purpose of the bill was to demonstrate that marijuana use presented a sufficiently serious health problem to warrant a reversal of the constitutional protection recognized in the Ravin decision. Although the Bill passed in the Senate it did not come to a vote in the House because expert testimony given during hearings regarding the Bill (CCSB 32) demonstrated that the claims made in SB 32 were inaccurate and would be thrown out in court.

Legislation to recriminalize marijuana was reintroduced in the Alaska Senate (SB 18) early in the 1989 session and was passed by a vote of 16-2 on March 22, 1989. The Bill makes possession of up to 8 ounces of marijuana by adults a misdemeanor, punishable by up to 90 days in jail and a $1,000 fine. The Senate bill continues to attempt to show that marijuana presents a danger to health which outweighs a person's right to privacy. The issue becomes one of whether this act, if passed by the House, would stand a court test. The Alaska State house is currently working on its own version of marijuana legislation which would make possession of marijuana by adults a violation punishable by a maximum $300 fine and no jail time.

What is interesting about the recent Senate Bill (SB 18) is that despite the zeal with which this legislation was sought by some legislators, the fiscal note accompanying it did not provide any additional funding for law enforcement, prosecution, court or prison expenses to accommodate the new legislation. Its prime sponsor, Senator Paul Fischer, said that "the intent is to send a message to the public that marijuana use is illegal, regardless of the number of arrests" (Persily, 1989, p. C3).

In summary, it is apparent that there is a definite need to clarify the state's public policy concerning marijuana. This issue is particularly important because given the youthful population of the state and the conflicting attitudes that people have toward drugs, especially marijuana, the lack of a definitive public policy can have an adverse influence on public education and prevention programs and policies, on intervention programs, and on the justice system.

The current controversy in Alaska concerning marijuana has implications for other states seeking to decriminalize marijuana use. The Alaska experience has become the basis for arguments for or against recriminalization, and the results of the 1983 studies (Segal 1983a, 1983b) have been cited to indicate that legalization of marijuana leads to an increase in its use. Such conclusions drawn from these data are unwarranted and unjustified because there are many confounding factors beyond the Ravin decision that have influenced drug-taking behavior in Alaska. Some of these factors are described above. A discussion of the implications concerning the Ravin decision and drug-taking behavior is found in Chapter 7.

The data presented in the following chapters describe the prevalence of drug-taking behavior among a special population in Alaska (youth in grades 7-12), whose use of any drug is illegal because they are minors. Using this information to argue for or against recriminalization of marijuana would be inappropriate.

Chapter 3

Method

OVERVIEW

The current research (conducted during 1977-1988, and referrred to as the *1988 study*), was undertaken as part of an effort to continue to monitor drug-taking behavior by Alaskan youth. This research is the second study in Alaska reporting on drug use and related information on youth in grades 7-12. It was designed to obtain information on the use or nonuse of drugs ranging from legal, socially sanctioned drugs for those of legal age (i.e., alcohol and tobacco), to illegal and unsanctioned drugs, such as marijuana, cocaine, stimulants, hallucinogens, depressants, inhalants, heroin, and tranquilizers, taken for social or recreational purposes.

RESEARCH DESIGN AND PROCEDURES

Given the special problems that Alaska presents in terms of accessibility it was decided (in the previous and current studies), that schools located in regional centers in the urban and rural areas of the state would provide an appropriate representative sample of secondary school students. This decision was based on the following reasons: (1) the communities that were picked are geographically and ethnically different and encompass the major regions of the state; and (2) about 65 percent of the school age population reside within the boundaries of the school districts selected.

The sampling procedure which provided a satisfactory means of obtaining representative data, and which allowed for cooperative planning with school districts, is area cluster sampling, a technique that takes advantage of the fact that the state is subdivided into several different areas. Area sampling permits sampling within given areas, such as cities within regions; the cluster component is a procedure that allows elements of the sample to be chosen from the population in groups or clusters instead of singly. In the present study the clusters are the preexisting junior and senior high schools within a given district—which is itself within a given geographical district of the state. This procedure ideally allows generalization of results from the sample to the larger population (Moser & Kalton, 1971). Additionally, depending on the specific features of the sampling plan in relation to the object of the assessment procedures, cluster sampling can be as efficient on a per-case basis as is simple random sampling (Selltiz, Jahoda, Deutsch, & Cook, 1967). Moreover, once the population being sampled is defined, random or non-random sampling procedures could be used to get the wanted sample.

Because Alaska has been divided into several major geographical regions by the state government for administrative purposes, and as each of these regions contains an urban center, each of these regional centers constituted a specific sampling area in which cluster sampling was undertaken. Six regional areas, containing the total of mainland Alaska, excluding the Aleutian Chain, were picked to constitute the sampling areas. The initial study, conducted during 1981-82, used a total of eight school districts to serve as clusters. These school districts were located in the following communities: Anchorage, Barrow, Bethel, Fairbanks, Juneau, Kotzebue, Nome, and Sitka.

The present study expanded the geographical areas to include two other school districts, Cordova and Seward, resulting in a broader representation of Alaskan youth. The results are thus presented in two principle ways: (1) an aggregation of findings from all ten districts, which provides a description of current drug-taking behavior; and (2) a comparison of the current findings with eight districts sampled in the original study (Segal, 1983).

The present survey procedure involves two different methods, each contingent on a school district's approach to having students respond to a questionnaire, and on the size of the junior-senior school populations. The different survey procedures are either: (1)

random sampling of students in grades 7-12, or (2) assessing the entire population of students in grades 7-12.

Approval first had to be obtained from each of the district's school board. The sampling procedure and format of the survey were derived by working with school administrators in each district. Some districts interpreted the drug survey as extracurricular, and allowed only those students who had parental consent to volunteer to participate in the study. In such cases samples were drawn from the body of students that had obtained parental consent. The number of refusals, however, amounted to fewer than 1.0 percent, a level that did not make any difference in the study. Other districts considered the research to be a legitimate school function that was consistent with their drug education curriculum. These districts did not call for parental consent and allowed the students to decide for themselves whether to participate in the study. The questionnaires were administered during school hours either by school personnel or by the principal investigator.

SAMPLING

As described above, the state is divided into several regions so that schools could be sampled within each region in a manner representative of total students enrolled in that region. In those locations where there was only one junior and senior high school, all students present on a given day were surveyed. In such cases the actual population of students in grades 7-12 was surveyed. For purposes of this report, however, the data gotten from an entire school district are treated as sample data.

When school districts contained more than one junior or senior high school, random stratification sampling was used to get adequate representation of men and women within grade levels in the different schools. The samples were not stratified for ethnic representation. It was thought that random sampling would provide a representation of racial and ethnic groups proportionate to their representation in the general school population. A listing of the sampling procedure for each school district and the number of students participating in the survey is found in Table 3-1.

The total sample resulted in 4,129 students in grades 7-12 from

TABLE 3-1. Sample Representation: 1987-1988 (n = 4129)

School District	Type of Sample	Males	Females	NR*	Total	Response Rate
Barrow	Total District	42.5%	54.8%	2.4%	146	
Cordova	Total District	55.1%	44.9%		118	
Fairbanks	Stratified	56.7%	43.8%	0.2%	836	57.7%
Juneau	Stratified	47.6%	52.2%	0.2%	418	70.0%
Sitka	Total District	47.1%	52.0%	0.9%	537	
Seward	Total District	51.8%	48.2%		197	
Kotzebue	Total District	54.4%	45.3%	0.3%	298	
Bethel	Total District	47.0%	52.6%	0.4%	230	
Nome	Total District	55.4%	44.6%		202	
Anchorage	Stratified	49.3%	50.7%		1147	76.5%

*No Response

ten school districts: Anchorage, Barrow, Bethel, Cordova, Fairbanks, Juneau, Kotzebue, Nome, Seward, and Sitka. Table 3-2 provides a description of the characteristics of this sample.

Eight Comparison School Districts: 1987-1988

Table 3-3 provides a description of the characteristics of the students from the eight communities that are matched with the 1983 findings. These are: Anchorage, Barrow, Bethel, Fairbanks, Juneau, Kotzebue, Nome, and Sitka.

Characteristics of the 1983 Baseline Study

Since comparisons will be made with the major findings from the first drug-use study conducted during 1981 and 1982, a description of the initial sample is provided in Table 3-4. The baseline study, however, did not include ethnicity in the questionnaire, thereby precluding comparison on this variable.

TABLE 3-2. Sample Characteristics — Ten School Districts: 1987-1988

Gender	n	Percent
Males	2097	50.8
Females	2018	48.9
Unreported	14	.3

Ethnicity*	n	Percent	Relative Percent
Alaska Native	721	17.5	20.2
American Indian	73	1.8	2.0
Asian-Pacific	113	2.7	3.2
Black	129	3.1	3.6
Hispanic	77	1.9	2.2
White	2277	55.1	63.9
Other	175	4.2	4.9
Not reported	564	13.6	

Grade	n	Percent
7	578	14.0
8	977	23.7
9	502	12.2
10	810	19.6
11	505	12.2
12	757	18.3

	Grade						
	7	8	9	10	11	12	Total
Males	314	513	240	414	259	358	2097
Females	263	462	255	393	246	399	2018
Total	577	975	495	807	504	757	4115

Age	n	Percent	Relative Percent
10	1	0.0	0.0
11	29	0.7	0.7
12	282	6.8	6.9
13	680	16.5	16.7
14	720	17.4	17.7
15	625	15.1	15.4
16	676	16.4	16.6
17	646	15.5	15.9
18	383	9.3	9.4
19+	27	0.7	0.7
NR**	60	1.4	

* Sitka not included.   **Not reported.

TABLE 3-3. Sample Characteristics — Eight Comparison Districts: 1987-1988

Gender	n	Percent	
Male	1930	50.6	
Female	1870	40.0	
Unreported	14	0.4	

Ethnicity*	n	Percent	Relative Percent
Alaska Native	689	18.1	21.2
American Indian	66	1.7	2.0
Asian-Pacific	102	2.7	3.1
Black	122	3.2	3.8
Hispanic	76	2.0	2.3
White	2024	53.1	62.3
Native/White	79	2.1	2.4
Filipino	6	0.2	0.2
Other	87	2.3	2.7
Not reported	563	14.8	

Grade	n	Percent
7	522	13.7
8	909	23.8
9	461	12.1
10	762	20.0
11	451	11.8
12	709	18.6

				Grade			
	7	8	9	10	11	12	Total
Males	283	474	223	392	227	331	1930
Females	238	433	231	367	223	378	1870
Total	521	907	454	759	450	709	3800

Age	n	Percent	Relative Percent
10	1	0.0	0.0
11	24	0.6	0.6
12	240	6.3	6.4
13	620	16.3	16.5
14	670	17.6	17.8
15	587	15.4	15.6
16	620	16.3	16.5
17	591	15.5	15.7
18	376	9.9	10.0
19+	27	0.7	0.7
NR**	58	1.5	

* Sitka not included. **Not reported.

TABLE 3-4. Sample Characteristics — Eight Comparison Districts: 1983

Gender	n	Percent
Males	1770	49.0
Females	1732	48.0
Unreported	107	3.0
Total	3609	

Grade	n	Percent
7	665	18.4
8	685	19.0
9	603	16.7
10	658	18.2
11	564	15.6
12	345	9.6
NR*	89	2.5

	7	8	Grade 9	10	11	12	Total
Males	318	321	294	322	318	186	1759
Females	337	355	303	332	241	154	1722
Total	655	676	597	654	559	340	3481
Unreported							128

Age	n	Percent	Relative Percent
11	2	0.1	0.1
12	202	5.6	5.9
13	633	17.5	18.4
14	623	17.3	18.1
15	611	16.9	17.8
16	610	16.9	17.8
17	482	13.4	14.0
18	254	7.0	7.4
19	16	0.4	0.5
NR*	176	4.9	

*Not Reported

THE QUESTIONNAIRE

A self-administered questionnaire was used to get information about use or nonuse of drugs. The questionnaire which was similar in content to the one used in the 1981-1982 study (referred to as the *1983 study*), but formatted differently, was pilot tested to assess its reliability and to confirm that its wording was consistent with a seventh grade reading level. The instrument demonstrates sufficient content validity to assure that it adequately assessed use or nonuse of drugs, and the nature and extent of drug use by those students reporting having tried a drug (Segal, 1983a). The new questionnaire was also reviewed by each school district which had the option to make revisions or to add questions to obtain specific information that was of interest to them. Few changes, except for Nome, were made. The questionnaire used in Nome involved changing individual questions about use or nonuse of drugs into matrix form. The two types of questionnaires are presented in Appendixes.

The only exception to the utilization of the revised questionnaire for the 1987-88 study was the Sitka School District. That district, before the inception of the present research project, conducted its own self-study of drug use and chose to use a modified 1981-1982 questionnaire. The district released its questionnaires to CAAS for evaluation and for inclusion in the follow-up study. Results describing aggregated data, therefore, will not always include items from Sitka because the Sitka measure was not totally comparable. The Sitka questionnaire is found in Appendix 3.

Each of the three questionnaires contained sets of items designed to obtain the information listed below:

1. *Demographic.* This section included questions that asked about gender, ethnic background, age, participation in drug education programs, grades achieved, and length of time lived in community.
2. *Drug Usage.* Information on drug usage included an extensive set of questions on nonprescriptive or social/recreational use of marijuana, cocaine, crack, stimulants, hallucinogens, depressants, heroin, inhalants, and tranquilizers, with specific reference to recency and frequency of use, problems resulting from use, age of first use, and estimates of level of peer use.
3. *Alcohol.* This section included information about the quantity and frequency of consumption, and about some adverse consequences of drinking.
4. *Tobacco.* Information on cigarette smoking and on use of smokeless tobacco products, including the quantity and frequency of use.
5. *Personality Items.* The use or nonuse of drugs is in part influ-

enced by personality characteristics. The incorporation of a measure of personality attributes facilitated an evaluation of what personality traits are related to use or nonuse of drugs.

CONFIDENTIALITY AND ANONYMITY

The purpose of the study was to gain an understanding of drug use among Alaskan youth, not to identify individuals who use drugs. In an effort to acquire reliable answers from the students, precautions were taken to protect their confidentiality and anonymity. The students' names were not asked for in any phase of the research. The only identifying information requested on the survey was age, ethnicity, gender and grade; no birthdate was requested. All students that were eligible were asked to volunteer to participate in the study. Few refused to participate when asked. In some locations students actively supported the study, viewing it as a means of helping their school combat drug use.

In addition to protecting the anonymity of students, the confidentiality of the school districts was also protected. In accordance with an agreement with each district no findings specific to the school district would be disclosed—each district would have the option of releasing its findings. No school districts are identified in this document. Findings will be reported as aggregated data either representative of the total sample or school districts grouped together to form regional samples. No community will be singled out when regional comparisons are made.

Data Checking

All the data obtained were entered into a computer file for detailed analysis. Before entry, each questionnaire was checked for inconsistencies or improbable response patterns. Questionnaires which contained partial or indistinct responses were corrected when possible. Any improperly completed questionnaires, or those with incomplete pages, were discarded. After each school district's data were entered into a computer data file, the file was screened to check for inaccuracies by determining if any responses were out of range for the questions asked, or for inconsistent responses.

Return Rate (Completion Rate)

A total of 4,381 questionnaires were returned to the Center for Alcohol and Addiction Studies from the ten school districts surveyed. After the checking process, 252 were discarded for any of the reasons cited above, resulting in a return or completion rate of 94.2 percent, which exceeded a minimal level of 90 percent. A total of 4,129 completed questionnaires were therefore entered into the 1987-1988 system file for statistical analysis. Any results reported for the 1987-1988 study are based on this figure unless otherwise stated.

Data Analysis

SPSSX system files were formed on the University's Digital Vax 8800 computer, running the VMS operating system, version 4.7. Analyses of the data were undertaken using SPSSX programs (SPSS, 1988).

Because the research involved disproportionate samples, prevalence data were obtained by using weighted and unweighted statistical analyses. A weighted analysis adjusts for differences in sample sizes by computing means and percentages based on their exact representation of the population sampled, except for sampling error. It is therefore possible to adjust for the differences in sample sizes among the ten different school districts. Weighting was accomplished by using the SPSSX "weight command," identifying each community as the weighting variable. The results section contains a comparison between weighted and unweighted findings.

Chapter 4

Results: Part I
Total Sample

OVERVIEW

This chapter reports the results of the survey asking about social/recreational (nonmedicinal) drug use by students in grades 7-12 conducted during 1987/88. Information compiled from over 4,000 students through a comprehensive questionnaire can be very extensive. There are many ways to analyze and report the results. Some may have either special or unique significance while others may be too general to be of value. It is therefore necessary to place limits on the reporting of the findings with the aim of presenting data that would be best used by researchers, schools, health planners, and governmental agencies.

The results are divided into three sections. This chapter reports the findings from the total sample, representing an aggregation of the ten school districts. The following chapter reports the results of comparison between the 1983 and 1988 findings. Chapter 6 provides a comparison of the Alaskan data with findings from other states and with data from national studies.

The results in this chapter are grouped into three categories: (A) *prevalence data*, which describe the type, extent, pattern, and frequency of drug-taking behavior, (B) *demographic characteristics*, which describe the association between prevalence and specific characteristics of the sample, such as the relationship between gender and drug use, and (C) some *correlates of drug use*, which describe some factors that may be viewed as either cause or consequences of drug use.

The data are presented in both tabular and graphic form. In some figures the name of each substance has been abbreviated. The following is a list of the abbreviations to help interpret the data when the findings are presented graphically: MJ = Marijuana, CK = Cocaine, CR = Crack, ST = Stimulants, HL = Hallucinogens, DP = Depressants, HR = Heroin, IN = Inhalants, TQ = Tranquilizers, AL = Alcohol, and TB = Cigarettes.

A. PREVALENCE AND PATTERNS OF DRUG-TAKING BEHAVIOR

1. Opportunity to Try Drugs

Drugs cannot be experienced unless there is an opportunity to try them. Data addressing the opportunity to try drugs convey an indication of the availability of drugs, what trends in use may be present and, by extrapolation, information about the extent which those who have a chance to try a drug do so. Figure 4-1 describes how many adolescents in the sample indicated having had an opportunity to try any of the different chemical substances, except for alcohol and tobacco. Both weighted and unweighted results are provided in the table. The sample was weighted to adjust for differences in community representation.

A comparison of the actual (unweighted) and projected (weighted) findings shows that the differences between them tend to be small, suggesting that the actual sample is representative of the population sampled, except for sampling error. The following discussion is therefore based on the unweighted or actual sample results, as is the interpretation of other findings unless noted otherwise.

What can be observed from the data in Figure 4-1 is that opportunity to try different chemical substances is pervasive, but with some variations. Marijuana is the drug most in evidence (70.1 percent), followed by inhalants (44.9 percent). Just less than two-fifths (39.3 percent) of the sample reported an opportunity to try cocaine. Stimulants are next, with 36.4 percent of the sample having indicated an opportunity to try them. Reports on the opportunity to try the remaining substances are less extensive, but over a quarter of the sample had an opportunity to try hallucinogens (23.1 percent), and

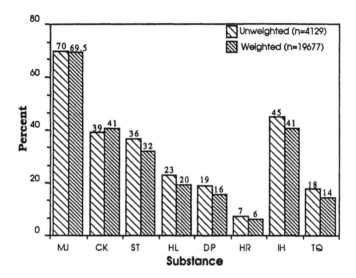

FIGURE 4-1. Opportunity to Try Chemical Substances Weighted and Un-weighted Comparison, Total Sample, 1988 (Figures are rounded to nearest whole.)

less than a fifth indicated a chance to try depressants (18.6 percent) or tranquilizers (17.6 percent). Last among the opportunity to try was heroin, with 7.4 percent of the sample noting an opportunity to try it.

2. Opportunity to Try and Trying a Drug

An important piece of information related to the opportunity to try a drug is the number of students who did try a substance when the chance arose. Table 4-1 reports the percent of students who indicated that they tried a substance when they had an opportunity. As noted from the data, except for crack and heroin, over half the students tried one of the substances when an opportunity occurred. Consistent with its level of apparent availability, three-quarters (75.9 percent) of those who had an opportunity to try marijuana did so. Stimulants are the next highest tried substance, with two-thirds (66 percent) of the sample showing that they tried it when a chance arose. Over half of those who had a chance to try cocaine (52 per-

TABLE 4-1. Opportunity to Try and Trying Drugs, Total Sample, 1988 ($n = 4129$)

Substance	Percent	n^a
Marijuana	75.9	2894
Cocaine[b]	52.2	295
Crack	29.0	348
Stimulants	66.0	1504
Hallucinogens	56.7	953
Depressants	50.6	770
Heroin	30.0	304
Inhalants	57.1	1855
Tranquilizers	54.3	728

[a]n equals the number of students reporting an opportunity to try each drug. It seves as the denominator from which the percent figure is derived.
[b]Includes Crack.

cent), hallucinogens (56.7 percent), depressants (50.6 percent), inhalants (57.1 percent), or tranquilizers (54.3 percent), tried them.

Based on the findings reported in Figure 4-1 and in Table 4-1, opportunities to try drugs existed in varying degrees, and over half the adolescents who had a chance to try a drug apparently tried it.

3. Lifetime Experience with a Chemical Substance (Lifetime Prevalence)

Figure 4-2 shows the findings related to the percent of students who reported ever having tried any of the substances one or more times during their lifetime (except for alcohol and tobacco). Both weighted and unweighted percentages are presented. The differences between the two sets of figures are relatively small, suggesting that the unweighted sample is representative of the sample population.

As can be observed, over half the students (53.2 percent) reported having tried marijuana at least once during their lifetime. Marijuana is the substance that most students had an opportunity to

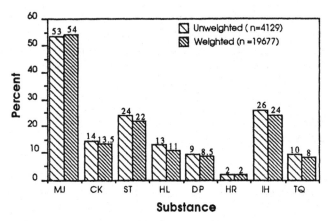

FIGURE 4-2. Lifetime Experience with a Chemical Substance Weighted and Unweighted Comparison, Total Sample, 1988

try and the one that most tried when presented with an opportunity to try it. Conversely, heroin which is the least available and least taken advantage of when an opportunity arose, is also least experienced. Of the remaining substances, inhalants are the second most experienced (25.7 percent), followed by stimulants (24.0 percent). Experiences with cocaine (14.4 percent) and hallucinogens (13.1 percent) are relatively comparable, but lower than marijuana, stimulants and inhalants. The prevalence of tranquilizers (9.6 percent) and depressants (9.4 percent) are also relatively comparable, but lower than cocaine and hallucinogens.

In summarizing the findings thus far, it appears that a pattern of use has emerged, one that revolves around using selected drugs to get what might be called a "cheap high." The three most tried substances, marijuana (a popularized mood altering drug taken to induce a pleasant feeling state), inhalants (cheap and available products such as gasoline), which also produce euphoria, and stimulants (relatively inexpensive substances which induce a high), are all euphoria-inducing substances. Cocaine and hallucinogens, substances that also induce a pleasant altered state of consciousness, are also used, but to a lesser extent. It is possible that their cost, together with a cautiousness about their use because of extensive publicity about their dangers, may be mitigating against more extensive use. Of the remaining substances, depressants and tranquil-izers, possibly because of cost and because neither is a particularly good euphoria-inducing drug, are not used extensively. Heroin and crack, which were least experienced, may either be unavailable, costly, or perceived as substances to avoid.

4. Lifetime Experience and 95 percent Confidence Intervals

Table 4-2 presents the lower and upper confidence intervals for the statistics describing lifetime experience with a drug reported in Figure 4-2. The data represent the unweighted sample figures. The confidence intervals have been included to show the range around which the actual population value may lie 95 out of one hundred times ($p < .05$).

5. Lifetime Experience: Percent of Students Having Tried One or More Drugs

Of the total 1988 sample of 4,129 students, 59.9 percent, or three-fifths of the students surveyed, reported having tried one or

TABLE 4-2. Lifetime Experience with a Chemical Substance with 95% Confidence Intervals Unweighted Frequencies, Total Sample, 1988 ($n = 4129$)

Substance	Lower Limit*	Percent	Upper Limit*
Marijuana	51.7	53.2	54.7
Cocaine**	13.3	14.4	15.5
Stimulants	22.7	24.0	25.3
Hallucinogens	12.0	13.1	14.2
Depressants	8.5	9.4	10.4
Heroin	1.7	2.0	2.4
Inhalants	24.4	25.7	27.0
Tranquilizers	8.6	9.6	10.6

*95% Confidence Intervals.   **Includes Crack.

more drugs at least once during their lifetime. Although lifetime prevalence is high, it needs to be noted that lifetime experience includes students who tried a drug once and stopped, and those who had used more than one substance more than one time, without accounting for recency of use.

6. Past Year Experience

The above findings change dramatically when experience *during the past year* is reported. Less than a quarter of the sample (21.8 percent) indicated having experienced one or more substances during the past year.

7. Past Month Experience

A further large decrease is noted for *past month use*, with less than ten percent (7.3 percent) of the students having indicated using a drug during this time period.

As noted above, different prevalence rates result when different time periods are referenced. Lifetime experience yields the highest prevalence because it includes all forms of use, experimental or regular, during a student's lifetime. Past year use provides a more recent picture which does not include students who experimented with drugs more than a year ago and stopped, or who were more frequent users but also stopped. What the findings show is that a large difference is found between the proportion of students who ever tried a drug and those who had a more recent drug experience. This difference becomes even more pronounced with respect to use during the past month. These data provide an estimate of students who are actively involved in drug use, which amounts to less than 10 percent (7.3 percent) of the sample.

8. Number of Drugs Tried

Figure 4-3 describes how many students tried one or more drugs. Inspection of the data shows that the largest percentage of students who had experiences with drugs restricted their experience to only one drug (39.6 percent). The proportion of students who experienced two or more drugs decreases steadily thereafter. A quarter of

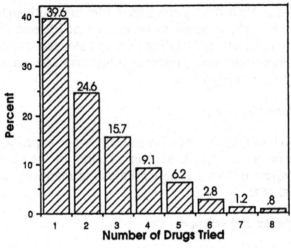

FIGURE 4-3. Number of Drugs Tried Among Students Having Tried, 1988 (n = 2475)

the sample (24.6 percent) experienced two drugs while 15.7 percent tried three drugs. Less than 10 percent four drugs (9.1 percent), and a total of ten percent (10.2 percent) tried 5 to 7 drugs. Less than 1 percent of the total sample (0.8 percent) indicated having experienced all eight of the drugs listed in the survey.

9. Drugs Experienced

Thus far the discussion has been reporting students' experience with one or more drugs. Figure 4-4 shows the actual number (frequency) of students who tried a single substance to the exclusion of others. Inspection of the data shows that the largest number of students (n = 1,023) limited their experience to marijuana. About an equal number restricted their experience to having tried stimulants (n = 570) or inhalants (n = 548) which rank second and third, respectively. Least tried were crack (n = 40) and heroin (n = 31). Experiences with cocaine, hallucinogens, depressants, and tranquilizers, are comparable. The overall configuration generally follows the pattern of use described for lifetime experience.

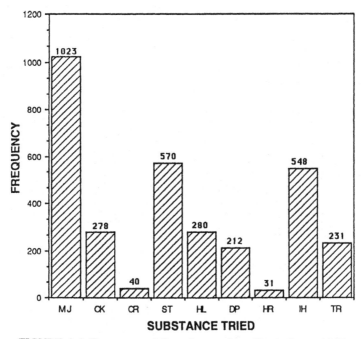

FIGURE 4-4. Frequency of Experience with a Single Drug, 1988

10. Past Year Experience

Figure 4-5 shows the distribution of reports of the frequency of use of seven different chemical substances tried during the past year. Heroin, because of its low prevalence, is not included. The figures in the legend next to each drug listed represent the actual number of respondents who indicated having tried each of the substances during the past year.

First among the findings is that experimentation (1-2 times) with the different substances appeared to have been the primary mode of use. Over 50 percent of the students tried either cocaine or tranquilizers once or twice while close to 50 percent tried either stimulants, hallucinogens, depressants, or inhalants. Interestingly, marijuana (< 35 percent) was the least experimented with drug. Between 30 percent and 35 percent of the students used drugs between 3 and 9 times, and after that the report of use begins to decline, a finding

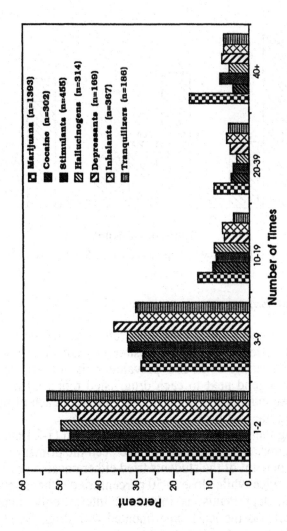

FIGURE 4-5. Past Year Experience with Chemical Substances, 1988

consistent with Thompson et al. (1985). Also of interest is the pattern of use. There is a clear trend of less experimentation and more frequent use of marijuana, with about 15 percent of the sample indicating having used marijuana more than 40 times during the past year. In contrast, there is greater experimentation with the other substances and less frequent use. About ten percent of those who tried a substance, however, tend to have been frequent users of any of the drugs listed in the figure.

11. Past Month Experience

Figure 4-6 presents the same information as in Figure 4-5 but shows the frequency of use during the past month. The findings show that drugs were used recently, and generally follow the pattern found in Table 4-5. Of particular significance in this Table is that about five percent of the students appear to be active and moderately heavy (20-39 times) or heavy (40+ times) users of marijuana, inhalants and tranquilizers. The latter figure represents greater than daily use of drugs by some students.

12. Experience by Grade Level

Figures 4-7 to 4-9 present findings related to grade level and drug use.

a. Prevalence by Grade Level

Figure 4-7 shows a comparison of weighted and unweighted results of the percent of students, *from among the entire sample;* who have tried one or more drugs (except alcohol and tobacco) *either before or during* the time they reached their current grade level. The data were weighted to account for differences in grade levels among the school districts. Although there are some small differences between the weighted and unweighted data, the overall pattern is nevertheless similar. What is shown is a pattern of use in which grades 8, 10, and 12 show higher prevalence levels than students in grades seven, nine, and eleven. More specifically, prevalence levels are lowest in grade 7, rise in grade 8, decrease in grade 9, increase again in grade 10, decrease in grade 11, and in-

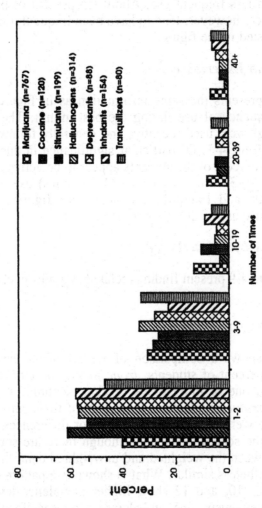

FIGURE 4-6. Past Month Experience with Chemical Substances, 1988

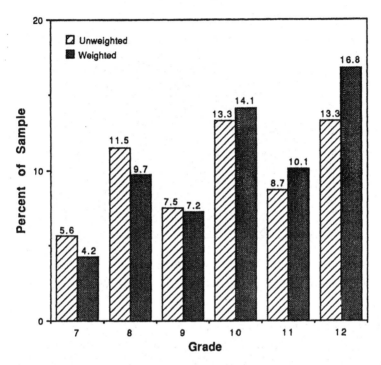

FIGURE 4-7. Lifetime Experience and Grade Level Comparison of Weighted and Unweighted Results, Total Sample, 1988

crease in grade 12. It appears that students may be at higher risk for drug use within grades 8, 10, and 12 than in grades 7, 9, and 11.

b. Prevalence Within Grade Levels

The data in Figure 4-8, which are based on a weighted sample to account for differences in the number of students within grade levels, represents the percent of students *within each grade level* who reported having tried a drug (i.e., the percent of students among all seventh graders who tried a drug). Figure 4-8 shows a different pattern of drug use for grade level than found in Figure 4-7 because the data for each grade level would total 100 percent if those not using drugs were included. This configuration indicates a direct relationship between grade and use — as grade level increases the

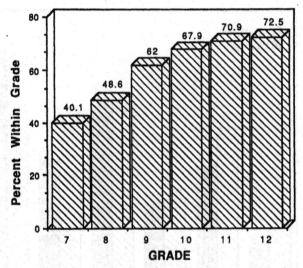

FIGURE 4-8. Lifetime Experience Within Grade Levels, Weighted Sample, 1988

number of students having tried increases. When students are in the ninth grade, or higher, at least three-fifths have tried a drug, and when students become high school seniors nearly three-quarters have tried one or more drugs.

c. Prevalence Within Grades
Among Those Having Tried a Drug

The data in Figure 4-9 is based on the proportion of students within each grade from among the total number of students in each grade who reported *ever having tried a drug*. The general configuration is similar to that shown in Figure 4-8.

13. Age of Initiation

Figures 4-10 through 4-13 present data related to age of initiation into drug-taking behavior for seven substances. Heroin and crack are not included because of their low prevalence rates. Figure 4-10 shows the ages of initiation for the seven substances: marijuana (MJ), cocaine (CK), stimulants (ST), hallucinogens (HL), depressants (DP), inhalants (IH), and tranquilizers (TQ).

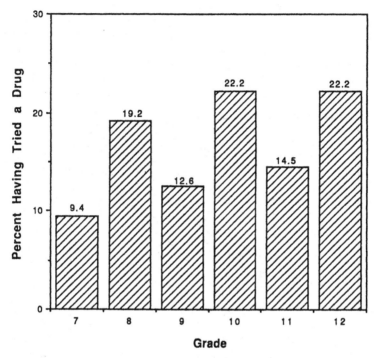

FIGURE 4-9. Lifetime Experience Within Grade Levels Among Students Having Tried a Drug, 1988 (*n* = 2475)

From this figure it appears that although some youth are begin-ning drug use at or before 11 years of age, the most common time for initiation into each type of drug is between 12 and 13 years. Except for inhalants which decrease after age 12, there is a sharp increase in initiation between 11 and 13 years. After that some drugs continue to peak, some decline while others show a brief plateau. Initiation into all substances begins to decline after age 15.

Figure 4-11 shows the same data Figure 4-10, but the ages are grouped into two-year intervals. The increase in initiation to age 13 is dramatically illustrated by the sharp rise in the slope of the line for each drug from less than 12 years to between 12-13 years. After that, initiation into hallucinogens and cocaine continues to increase very sharply. What is of particular concern is the large number of students (about 35 percent) who have tried inhalants before they are

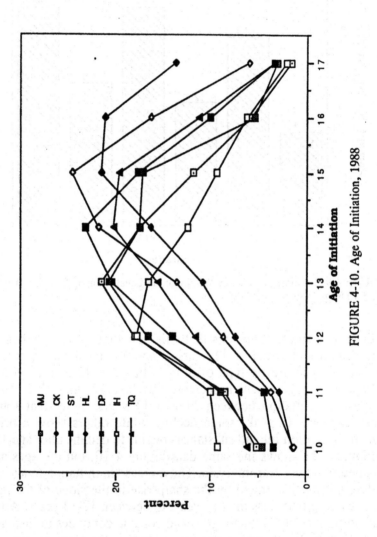

FIGURE 4-10. Age of Initiation, 1988

46

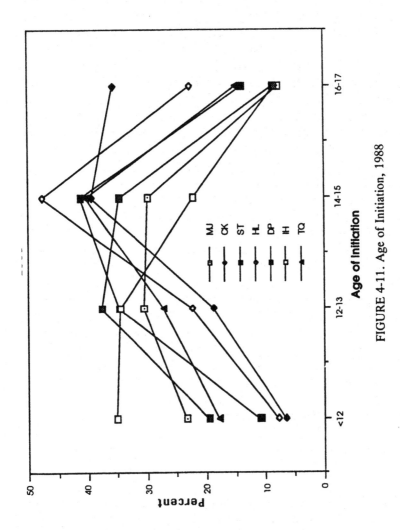

FIGURE 4-11. Age of Initiation, 1988

twelve. Over 20 percent of the students had also tried marijuana while initiation into depressants and tranquilizers is also high.

Figure 4-12 shows a direct comparison of the age of initiation by age groupings for marijuana, cocaine, stimulants and inhalants, the four most prevalent substances tried by members of the sample. What may be observed more clearly from this table is that while many students try inhalants at an early age (< 12), its initiation begins to decline after that. But, as initiation into inhalants declines, initiation into marijuana, stimulants, and cocaine increases. The most dramatic increase occurs for cocaine which rises sharply between 12-13 and 14-15 years, and stays high at 16-17 years. Marijuana use tends to stay steady between 12-13 and 14-15 years and then declines. Stimulant use also increases sharply to 12-13 years, slowly until 14-15 years, and then declines rapidly.

Shown in Figure 4-13 are initiation rates by age groupings for hallucinogens, depressants, and tranquilizers. Among these substances, use of hallucinogens show the most dramatic increase, peaking at 14-15 years then declining rapidly. Depressant use increases to 12-13 years, then begins to decline after that, while use of tranquilizers tends to show a steady increase up until age 14-15, and a rapid decline after that.

In summary of the findings on initiation into drug-taking behavior, the period between 12 and 13 years presents the greatest risk for initiation into or experimentation with drugs. After age 13, initiation continues to increase for some substances while it decreases for others. The major exception to this pattern is initiation into cocaine which peaks at age 15, and stays high through 17 years of age. It appears that students might have started to try cocaine after other substances were tried first. Also, there is a uniform trend showing a decrease in initiation after age 15.

14. Alcohol: Lifetime
and Past Year Prevalence

Findings about alcohol or drinking behavior among the sample have been separated from the results on other drugs in order to discuss it as a separate entity.

Figure 4-14 shows the proportion of students who had ever con-

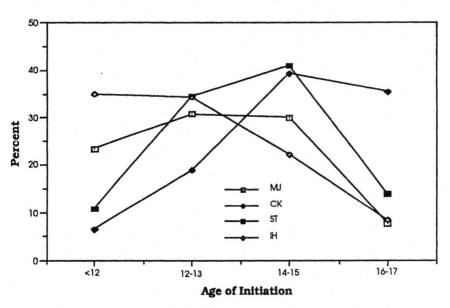

FIGURE 4-12. Age of Initiation, Marijuana-Cocaine-Stimulants-Inhalants, 1988

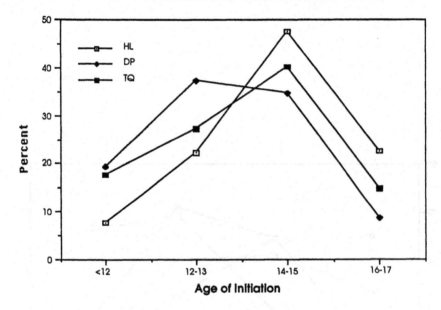

FIGURE 4-13. Age of Initiation, Hallucinogens-Depressants-Tranquilizers, 1988

sumed alcohol (beer, wine or whiskey) outside their home with friends, and the percent of students who had reported drinking alcoholic beverages during the past year. About three-quarters of the sample (74 percent) had indicated that they had consumed an alcoholic beverage during their lifetime, and close to two-thirds of the sample (58.4 percent) noted that they had consumed an alcoholic beverage during the past year.

15. Frequency of Drinking: Past 30 Days

Figure 4-15 shows the number of occasions students used alcohol during the past thirty days. The data in the table are derived from those students who reported ever having consumed alcohol ($n =$ 2292). It is apparent from the data in Figure 4-15 that most students who drank did so only 1-3 times (44.3 percent). Fewer (13.8 percent) drank 1-2 times a week, and fewer (6.8 percent) used alcohol 3-4 times a week. Cumulatively, 3.7 percent of the students drank more than 5-6 times a week. Thirty-one percent of the students reported that they did not drink any alcoholic beverages during the past 30 days.

16. Quantity of Drinking: Past 30 Days

Among those who drank during the past 30 days (n = 2633), the majority (35.9 percent), as shown in Figure 4-16, consumed 2-5 drinks. Over ten percent had 6-10 drinks while 7.1 percent had 11 or more drinks. About a third of the students (32.2 percent) did not drink while 11.6 percent had only one drink.

17. Alcohol and Grade Level

a. Percent of Sample

Figure 4-17 describes the percent of students, from among the total sample (based on unweighted data), who reported having consumed alcohol before or at their current grade level. The configura-

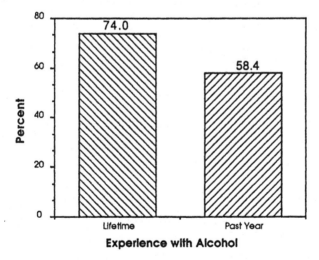

FIGURE 4-14. Experience with Alcohol, Total Sample, 1988 (n = 4129)

tion is identical to the pattern observed in Figures 4-7 and 4-9 for use of drugs. Grades 8, 10 and 12 all show peaks or increases while grades 7, 9 and 11 show decreases. The similarity of these findings reinforces the notion that some levels may be more critical than others for use of alcohol and other drugs.

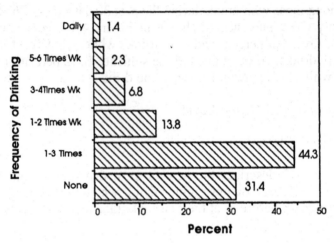

FIGURE 4-15. Frequency of Drinking Past Thirty Days, 1988 (n = 2962)

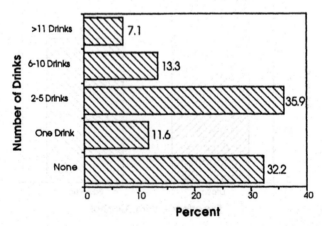

FIGURE 4-16. Amount of Drinks Consumed Past Thirty Days, 1988 (n = 2633)

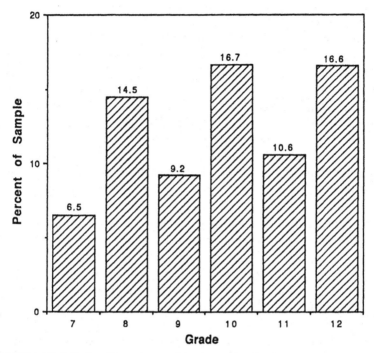

FIGURE 4-17. Lifetime Experience with Alcohol by Grade, Total Sample, 1988 (n = 4129)

b. Within Grade Levels

Figure 4-18 which reports lifetime prevalence with alcohol *within each grade level*, shows a similar configuration to that in Figure 4-8. Evident in this figure is that as grade level increases a greater proportion of students drink alcohol.

18. Cigarettes and Smokeless Tobacco

Figure 4-19 presents data on the prevalence of smoking cigarettes and on the use of chewing or smokeless tobacco. Slightly over three-fifths (61.9 percent) of the sample have smoked cigarettes, and over a third (38.4 percent) have tried either smokeless or chewing tobacco at least once.

19. Frequency of Smoking:
Past 30 Days

The frequency which students reported smoking is described in Figure 4-20. Interestingly, of those who reported ever having tried smoking, over half (55.5 percent) did not smoke during the past 30 days. Among those who did smoke, it appears that they can be divided into two primary groups, one which tends to smoke infrequently [less than 4 times a week (19.0 percent)] and a second which tends to be heavier smokers [two-three times a day or more (21.8 percent)].

20. Initiation into Alcohol, Cigarettes, and Smokeless Chewing Tobacco

A comparison of ages of initiation into alcohol, cigarettes, and smokeless or chewing tobacco is shown in Figure 4-21. A higher percentage of students are initiated into tobacco products than alcohol at ages 10 and 11, but then initiation into alcohol increases steadily until age 13, and decreases thereafter. Initiation into tobacco products declines steadily after peaking at 12 years of age. Although many students have reported smoking cigarettes or using smokeless or chewing tobacco (see Figures 4-19 and 4-20), their use appears to have its largest occurrence before age 13.

21. Initiation into Alcohol, Cigarettes and Marijuana

Figure 4-22 provides a comparison of age of initiation into alcohol, cigarettes and marijuana, three of the most widely-used substances by the students in the sample. Although more students started using cigarettes than either alcohol or marijuana at ages 10 to 11, its initiation declined very sharply after peaking at age 12, the age level when initiation into alcohol and marijuana starts to increase. Initiation into marijuana and alcohol peaks at 13 years, and then declines steadily. The initiation curves for alcohol and marijuana are almost alike, suggesting that their onset may be highly interrelated.

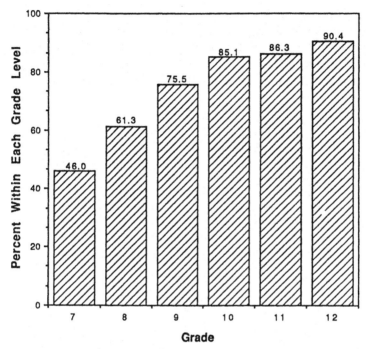

FIGURE 4-18. Lifetime Experience with Alcohol Within Grade Levels, 1988 (*n* = 3057)

SUMMARY

The nature and pattern of drug-taking behavior reported by the students in the sample tends to reflect high prevalence rates for experiences with chemical substances. More than half of the students reported having tried marijuana, nearly one in every three reported having tried stimulants or inhalants, and nearly one out of every five have tried cocaine. Experiences with other drugs are also high, including alcohol and tobacco products. What is evident is that when there was a chance to try a drug (although illicitly), over half of the students tried a drug. Although most experiences with chemical substances seem to be experimental, less than ten percent of the sample may be frequent or regular drug users. Many students have consumed alcohol, with about 70 percent actively drinking varying amounts with varying frequency. A large proportion of students have smoked cigarettes or tried smokeless or chewing tobacco, with about a quarter of the sample actively smoking.

There is also a definite relationship between age and grade and drug-taking behavior. As age and grade increase there is a corres-

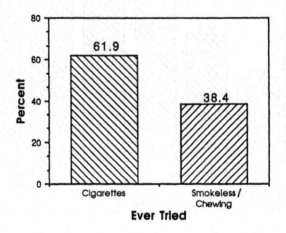

FIGURE 4-19. Use of Tobacco Products, Lifetime Experience, Total Sample, 1988 (*n* = 4129)

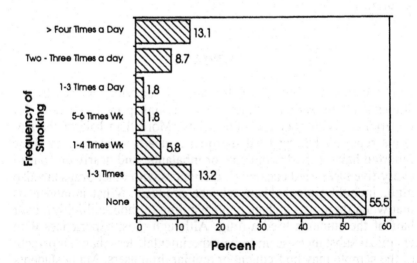

FIGURE 4-20. Frequency of Smoking Past Thirty Days, 1988 (*n* = 2381)

ponding increase in the prevalence of drug-taking behavior, but this relationship is more complex than it seems since it appears to vary with the age at which different drugs are first experienced. Nevertheless, ages 12 and 13 are the ages during which most drugs are most probably tried for the first time.

B. DEMOGRAPHIC CHARACTERISTICS AND DRUG USE

This section describes some relationships between prevalence and specific characteristics of the sample.

1. Gender and Drug Use

Among the students in the sample, more male respondents (52.3 percent) than female students (47 percent) tried a substance (excluding alcohol and tobacco) one or more times.

2. Gender and Drug Use Among Students Having Tried a Drug

Among those students who had reported ever having tried a drug, slightly more male respondents (31.1 percent) than female respondents (28.8 percent) tried one or more drugs.

3. Grade and Drug Use by Substance

The data in Figure 4-23 are based on the number of students among the total sample, at different grade levels, who ever tried a substance. Heroin and tranquilizers are not included because of their lower prevalence levels. The overall configuration generally follows the patterns of use reported earlier when describing grade and drug use, but varies for different drugs. One clear pattern involves cigarettes (TB), alcohol (AL), and marijuana (MJ), the substances showing the highest prevalence levels. Use, which is high in the seventh grade compared to inhalants (IH), stimulants (ST), depressants (DP), and cocaine (CK), increases at grade eight, then rises and falls after that. This same pattern is observed for the other

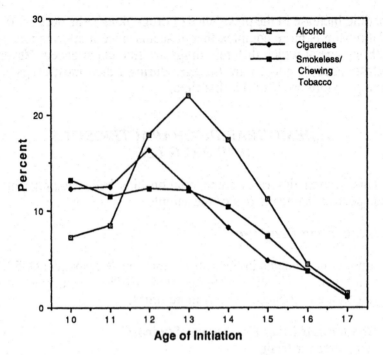

FIGURE 4-21. Age of Initiation, Alcohol-Cigarettes-Smokeless/Chewing Tobacco, 1988

substances, but at much lower prevalence levels, and with less dramatic increases and decreases. The general configuration not only continues to suggest that grades 8, 10, and 12 may be important periods related to drug-taking behavior, but also that use of some drugs stay consistent while use of others may either be low or minimal after initiation.

4. Grade, Gender, and Lifetime Experience with a Drug

The pattern of use observed in Figure 4-24 (which is based on the number of students within each grade who reported ever having tried a drug from among all students), illustrates the relationship

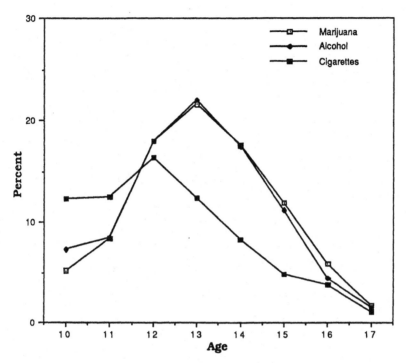

FIGURE 4-22. Age of Initiation, Alcohol-Cigarettes-Marijuana, 1988

between gender, grade, and experience with a drug. The findings are consistent with the data observed in Figure 4-17. Except for grades 9 and 11, where use is about equal, male students generally tried drugs to a greater extent than female students. This finding suggests that drug-taking behavior is not only age-grade related, but that gender may also be an important factor in understanding drug use among adolescents.

5. Ethnicity and Lifetime Experience
with a Drug: Total Sample

The data in Figure 4-25 describes lifetime experience with a drug by ethnicity from nine school districts. (Sitka, which did not ask

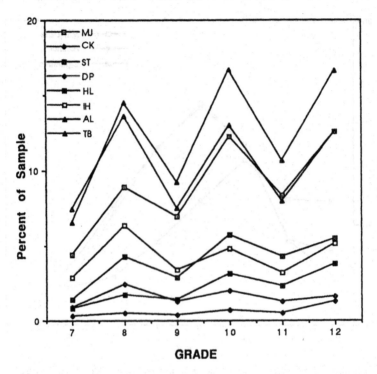

FIGURE 4-23. Lifetime Experience: Substance by Grade Level, Total Sample, 1988 (*n* = 4129)

ethnicity, is omitted from any analysis of ethnicity data.) As is readily observable, the largest proportion of students who tried a drug are White (36.5 percent), followed by Alaska Natives (15.0 percent). Drug use among the other groups is less than 2 percent, except for the "Other" category.

6. Lifetime Experience with a Drug Within Ethnic Groups

Figure 4-26 describes the number of students *within* each of the different ethnic groups who reported ever having tried a drug. Among those who identified themselves as either an Alaska Native or American Indian, close to 75 percent within each group (73.9

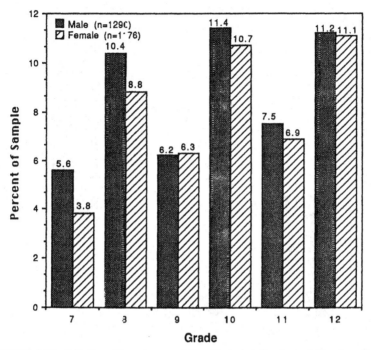

FIGURE 4-24. Lifetime Experience with a Drug by Grade and Gender, Total Sample, 1987-1988 (n = 4129)

percent and 72.6 percent, respectively), have indicated that they tried one or more substances. Over two-thirds of the Hispanic students (63.6 percent), and those in the "Other" (chiefly half Alaska Native and half White) category (62.3 percent), have also tried a drug. Less than half the Black students (41.1 percent) have tried a drug while close to two-thirds (57.2 percent) of the White students have indicated having tried a drug. Slightly over half of the Asian-Pacific students (51.3 percent) have indicated trying a drug.

7. Ethnicity and Lifetime Experience with Alcohol

The pattern of lifetime experience with alcohol, reported in Figure 4-27 follows that shown in Figure 4-26 for experiences with

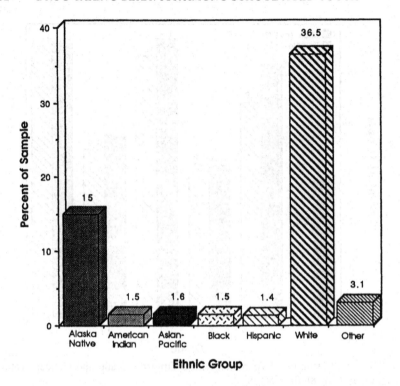

FIGURE 4-25. Ethnicity and Lifetime Experience with a Drug, Total Sample, 1988 (n = 3565) (Excludes Sitka)

other drugs. Whites show the highest prevalence (58.9 percent) while Alaska Natives are second (17.4 percent). Experience with alcohol among the other ethnic groups are comparable.

8. Ethnicity and Lifetime Experiences
with Chemical Substances

Figures 4-28 through 4-37 show lifetime experience *within* each of the different ethnic groups for each of the chemical substances, excluding heroin because of its low prevalence level.

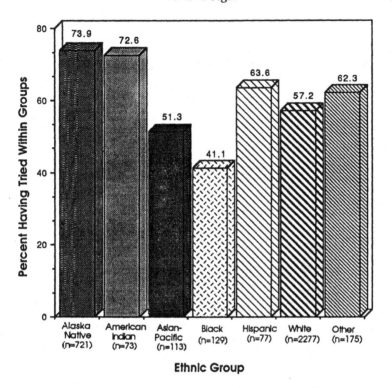

FIGURE 4-26. Drug Use Within Ethnic Groups, 1983 and 1988 (Excludes Sitka)

a. Marijuana

Figure 4-28 shows individual variations for use or nonuse of marijuana within ethnic groups. Among those groups having ever tried marijuana, Alaska Natives show the highest prevalence (71.3 percent), followed by American Indian (65.8 percent), and Hispanic (53.2 percent) students. Students classified as "Other" (largely students of mixed ethnic backgrounds), show the next highest prevalence level (44.6 percent). Just over half the White students (50.7 percent) tried marijuana, and less than half of the Asian-Pacific students tried marijuana (43.4 percent). Black Students showed the lowest prevalence (35.7 percent).

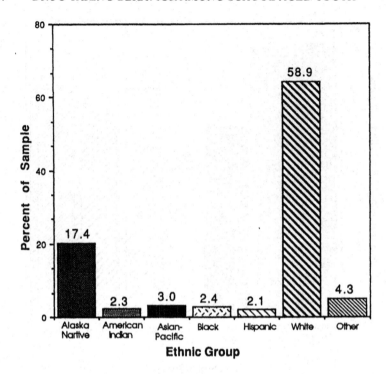

FIGURE 4-27. Ethnicity and Lifetime Experience with Alcohol, Total Sample, 1988 (*n* = 2657) (Excludes Sitka)

b. Cocaine

As is observable in Figure 4-29, the prevalence levels for experience with cocaine (including crack) are generally low across ethnic groups. Among those who have ever tried cocaine, Hispanics showed the highest level (6.5 percent), followed by White students (5.1 percent).

c. Stimulants

Among those ethnic groups trying stimulants (Figure 4-30) American Indian (39.7 percent) and Hispanics (37.7 percent) show the highest levels, followed by White students (26.7 percent). Black students show the lowest prevalence level (10.9 percent).

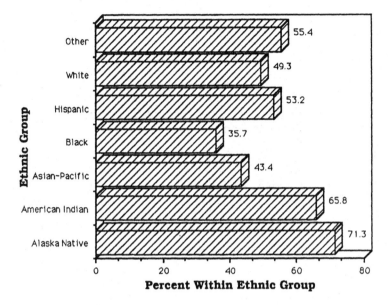

FIGURE 4-28. Ethnicity and Marijuana: Lifetime Experience, 1988 (Excludes Sitka)

d. Hallucinogens

The highest level of experience with hallucinogens, as shown in Figure 4-31, is among Hispanic students (24.7 percent), followed by American Indian (20.5 percent) and Whites (15.5 percent). Blacks show the lowest level (6.2 percent).

e. Depressants

Figure 4-32 shows that among students within the different ethnic groups reporting having tried depressants, Hispanics (24.7 percent) and American Indians (20.5 percent) show the highest prevalence levels. Whites are next (15.5 percent), followed by students in the "Other" category (13.7 percent). Blacks show the lowest level of use (6.2 percent), followed by Alaska Natives (8.7 percent).

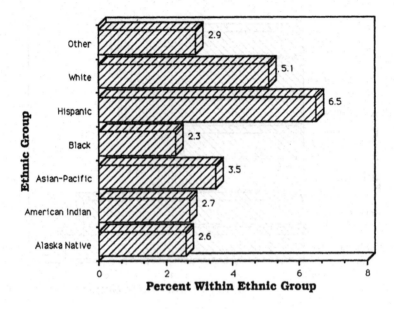

FIGURE 4-29. Ethnicity and Cocaine: Lifetime Experience, 1988 (Excludes Sitka)

f. Tranquilizers

Generally, lifetime prevalence for tranquilizers is low, as shown in Figure 4-33. Among those groups having tried it, Hispanics show the highest level (16.9 percent), followed by Whites (11.3 percent). Alaska Natives show the lowest use (5.1 percent), with Blacks (7.0 percent) having the next highest level.

g. Inhalants

Except for marijuana (Figure 4-28), lifetime prevalence for use of the other substances (Figures 4-29 to 4-33) is low. In contrast to these findings, lifetime experience with inhalants is proportionately higher across all ethnic groups, as shown in Figure 4-34. Inhalant use is most prevalent with the Hispanic (35.1 percent), American Indian (32.9 percent), and White (27.3 percent) groups. Alaska Natives (26.5 percent) and the group classified as "Other" (24.6 per-

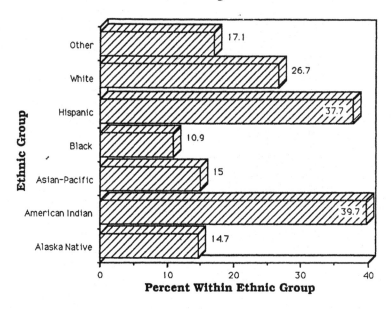

FIGURE 4-30. Ethnicity and Stimulants: Lifetime Experience, 1988 (Excludes Sitka)

cent) follow. Use among Blacks (13.5 percent) and Asian-Pacific (16.8 percent) students is also high when compared to their experiences with other substances.

h. Alcohol

Figure 4-35 describes lifetime experience with alcohol by ethnicity. The highest prevalence level is among American Indian youth (87.7 percent), followed closely by Hispanics (76.6 percent), Whites (75.1 percent) and Alaska Natives (74.5 percent). Blacks show the lowest level (58.1 percent).

i. Cigarettes

Figure 4-36 shows the findings regarding ethnicity and lifetime experience with cigarettes. American Indian (82.2 percent) and Alaska Native (81.4 percent) show the highest levels, followed by students in the "Other" group (79.4 percent) and Hispanic students

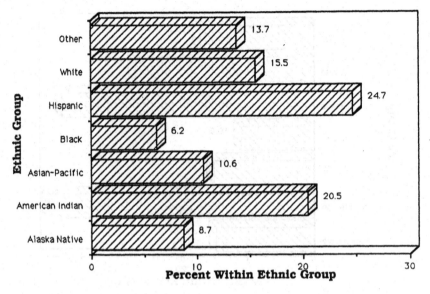

FIGURE 4-31. Ethnicity and Hallucinogens: Lifetime Experience, 1988 (Excludes Sitka)

(70.1 percent). Blacks show the lowest prevalence level (49.6 percent) followed by Asian-Pacific Islanders (59.3 percent). White students achieve a relatively high level, with 68.8 percent having reported smoking one or more times during their lifetime.

j. Chewing/Smokeless Tobacco

Chewing or smokeless tobacco has been used by many students within each of the ethnic groups (Figure 4-37). This finding is consistent with reports of an increase in smokeless tobacco use among adolescents during the past five years (Jones & Moberg, 1988; McCarthy et al., 1986). A particularly high prevalence level has been noted among Alaska Native youth (Tanner, 1987), a finding which is supported by this study. Alaska Native youth show the highest prevalence level (69.6 percent) for having tried either chewing or smokeless tobacco. Students in the "Other" ethnic category (53.7 percent) and American Indian youth (53.4 percent) both show the second highest levels for having tried/used smoking or chewing to-

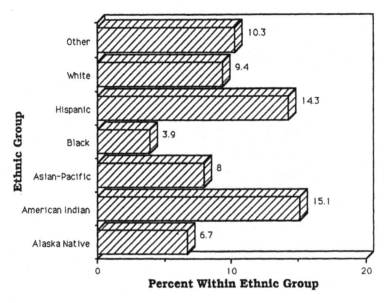

FIGURE 4-32. Ethnicity and Depressants: Lifetime Experience, 1988 (Excludes Sitka)

bacco. White youth follow, with 32.5 percent having indicated they tried chewing or smokeless tobacco, Hispanic youth are next (32.5 percent), followed by Asian-Pacific (23.9 percent) youth. Black students, in contrast to their smoking behavior, show the lowest prevalence level (20.2 percent) for having tried smokeless or chewing tobacco.

In summary of the findings about drug-taking behavior within ethnic groups, Hispanic and American Indian youth, who constitute 2.0 percent (n = 76) and 1.7 percent (*n* = 66) of the sample, respectively, show a disproportionately high level of prevalence for lifetime experience for all substances. Other ethnic groups show variations in their prevalence of drug-taking behavior. Some of these variations may be accounted for by cultural differences within each of the ethnic groups, and by peer influence or encouragement from a group of close friends who mutually support drug use and who use drugs together (Oetting, Edwards, & Beauvais, in press).

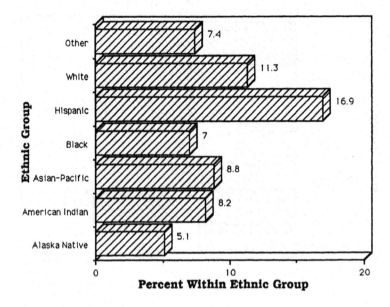

FIGURE 4-33. Ethnicity and Tranquilizers: Lifetime Experience, 1988 (Excludes Sitka)

C. CORRELATES: DRUG EXPERIENCES AND RELATED BEHAVIORS

1. Reasons for Not Trying Drugs (Excluding Alcohol and Tobacco)

Students who did not use drugs were asked to rank each of 11 reasons for not using a drug on a five-point scale ranging from "Very true of me" to "Not true of me." An analysis of the results shows the order in which each of the items were ranked:

Rank	Item
1	Not important for me to try
2	Fear of damage to mind
3	It is illegal
3	May cause addiction

3	Moral reasons
6	Disappoint my parents
7	Fear of bad experience
8	Because of something learned in school
9	No opportunity to try drugs
10	Pressure from friends
11	Knowing friends who had a bad trip

The rankings, which form an interesting array, show that the primary reason for not having tried a drug is that it is "Not important for me to try." The second most important reason for not trying is because of "Fear of damage to mind." Three reasons are tied for third place: "It is illegal," "May cause addiction," and "Moral reasons." Of least importance is "Knowing friends who had a bad trip," and "Pressure from friends." It appears that the decision to refrain from drug use appears to be more of a personal one than one influenced by peers. Concern over the adverse effects of drugs, and

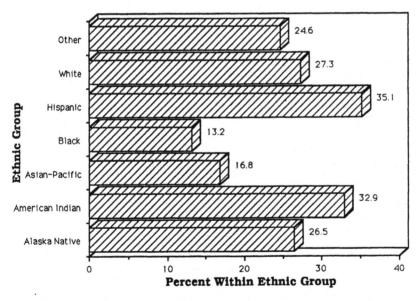

FIGURE 4-34. Ethnicity and Inhalants: Lifetime Experience, 1988 (Excludes Sitka)

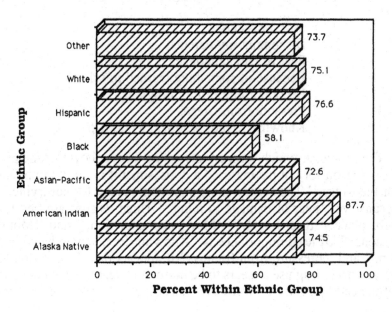

FIGURE 4-35. Ethnicity and Alcohol: Lifetime Experience, 1988 (Excludes Sitka)

the fact that it is illegal, seem to be very influential in a decision to not try a drug.

2. Consequences of Drug Use (Excluding Alcohol and Tobacco)

Students who reported ever having tried a drug were asked to indicate the frequency (ranging from never to 4 or more times) with which they may have experienced one of seven adverse effects. Listed below is the order of occurrence, ranging from *most* to *least* frequent occurrence, based on mean rank scores for each item.

Rank	Mean	Item
1	1.67	Had it get in the way of school work (n = 615)
2	1.51	Gotten into trouble with your friends (n = 560)

3	1.41	Had a bad trip (n = 507)
4	1.29	Gotten you in trouble with your teachers or principal (n = 333)
5	1.22	Gotten you in trouble with the police (n = 275)
6	1.19	Resulted in an accident or injury to you or others (n = 234)
7	1.14	Been suspended from school (n = 165)

Two of the most frequent adverse consequences of drug use are interference with academic achievement and contributing to difficulty with friends. Least experienced is suspension from school or having caused an injury to oneself or others, but many of the students did encounter trouble with the police or with school authorities.

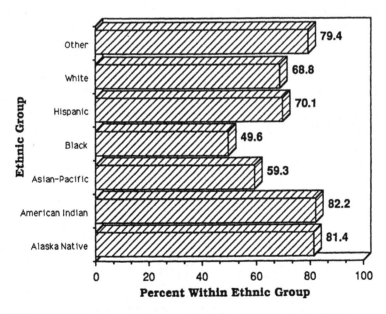

FIGURE 4-36. Ethnicity and Cigarette Smoking: 1988 (Excludes Sitka)

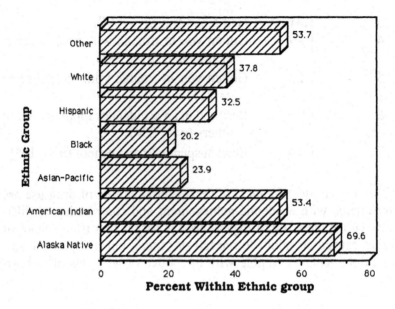

FIGURE 4-37. Ethnicity and Lifetime Experience with Chewing or Smokeless Tobacco, 1988 (Excludes Sitka)

3. *Consequences of Alcohol*

A set of questions also assessed the adverse consequences of drinking. Listed below is the order of occurrence, ranging from *most* to *least* frequent occurrence, based on mean rank scores for each item.

Rank	Mean	Item
1	1.43	Have driven when drinking ($n = 579$)
2	1.41	Gotten you in a fight ($n = 658$)
3	1.34	Gotten into trouble with your friends ($n = 509$)
4	1.27	Had it get in the way of school work ($n = 371$)
5	1.20	Gotten you in trouble with the police ($n = 350$)

6   1.17   Resulted in an accident or injury to you or others ($n = 196$)

7   1.09   Gotten you in trouble with your teachers or principal ($n = 159$)

The two highest ranked consequences of drinking have serious implications: drinking and driving and fighting while drinking. Drinking and driving, which places students at risk for injury, liability and arrest, have a very high prevalence level among adolescents (Evans, 1987; Millstein & Irwin, 1988; Simpson & Mayhew, 1987). The problem has been one of significant national concern to warrant special study (cf., Moskowitz, 1987; 1988).

The second most prevalent adverse consequence of drinking interrelates with the second ranked effect of drug use, interpersonal difficulty. The least adverse consequence for drinking is problems with teachers or a school's principal.

In reviewing the two sets of findings, it appears that the primary adverse effects of drugs other than alcohol is to interfere with school work while alcohol's chief adverse effect is drinking and driving. Common to both is difficulty with friends. These findings suggest that drinking may happen largely outside the school setting, thereby minimizing its impact within the school and possibly raising problems with friends. Use of other drugs may reflect the stronger toxic effect of illicit chemical substances which are known to interfere with cognitive processes (Newcomb & Bentler, 1988a).

SUMMARY

This chapter reported the findings from a 1987-1988 survey of drug-taking behavior among students in grades 7 to 12 in ten different school districts. The study shows generally high prevalence levels for lifetime experiences with different chemical substances, alcohol, tobacco, and chewing/smokeless tobacco. The general consistency of the findings suggests that the statistics reported have validity.

Chapter 5

Results: Part II
Comparing Findings in Alaska:
1983 and 1988

The findings reported in the previous chapter were obtained from a second stateside survey of drug-taking behavior among students in grades 7-12. The first survey was conducted during 1981 and 1982, and involved eight school districts (Anchorage, Barrow, Bethel, Fairbanks, Juneau, Kotzebue, Nome, and Sitka). This chapter provides a comparison of the major findings from the two surveys. The 1981-1982 data is called the 1983 study (Segal, 1983a). The current study is called the 1988 study.

A. COMPARISONS OF PREVALENCE
AND PATTERNS OF DRUG-TAKING BEHAVIOR

1. Opportunity to Try

Table 5-1 shows a comparison of *opportunities to try* chemical substances (marijuana, cocaine, stimulants, hallucinogens, depressants, heroin, inhalants, and tranquilizers). What is apparent is that opportunities to try the different substances, except for depressants, increase, some by small, others by large margins. Inhalants, for example, show the largest increase (19.4 percent), followed by more modest increases for hallucinogens (5.2 percent) and marijuana (4.3 percent). Depressants, in contrast, show a 1.1 percent decrease. The general pattern suggests that changes to try drugs have generally increased from five years ago. The results of a statistical test to determine if the differences between the proportions for each substance are statistically significant, indicate that some differences are greater than chance expectancy. The increases in opportunities to try marijuana, hallucinogens, inhalants, and tranquilizers, are all statistically significant.

2. Opportunity to Try and Trying Drugs

While students reported an increase in opportunities to try most drugs, the number of students who tried a drug (excluding alcohol and tobacco) when an opportunity arose has generally declined since 1983, as noted in Table 5-2. The largest decreases observed were for depressants (-20.2 percent) and tranquilizers (-18.0 percent), which are both statistically significant ($p = < .01$), that is, greater than chance expectancy. The declines for cocaine (-16.1 percent) and stimulants (-10.2 percent), were also statistically significant ($p < .01$). The small increase noted for marijuana ($+1.1$ percent) is not statistically significant, but the increase in hallucinogens ($+8.7$ percent) is greater than chance expectancy ($p < .01$).

3. Lifetime Experience with a Drug

Table 5-3 shows the pattern of increases and decreases for lifetime experience with different drugs (excluding alcohol and tobacco). Consistent with the findings in Tables 5-1 and 5-2, increases are noted for marijuana (3.6 percent) and hallucinogens (4.5 percent). A large increase for inhalants (9.4 percent) is also noted,

TABLE 5-1. Comparison of 1983 and 1988 Findings: Opportunity to Try Chemical Substances, Eight School Districts

Substance	1988 Percent[a]	1983 Percent[b]	Percent Change
Marijuana	70.4	66.1	+ 4.3[c]
Cocaine	30.5	29.0	+ 1.5
Stimulants	36.7	35.7	+ 1.0
Hallucinogens	23.3	18.1	+ 5.2[c]
Depressants	19.0	20.1	- 1.1
Heroin	7.5	7.2	+ 0.3
Inhalants	45.2	26.8	+ 18.4[c]
Tranquilizers	18.1	15.9	+ 2.2[c]

[a]N=3814 (Unweighted) [b]N=3609 (Unweighted) [c]$p < .01$.

which is consistent with its reported increase in availability reported in Table 5-1. All the differences in lifetime experience, except for heroin, are statistically significant. That is, the increases and decreases in lifetime experience that occurred, other than for heroin, are greater than chance expectancy.

Generally, the pattern of increases and decreases in Tables 5-1 through 5-3 indicates that marijuana continued to show the highest prevalence level. The increase in inhalants and hallucinogens suggests a possible trend away from more expensive, traditionally "hard" drugs (e.g., cocaine) to less expensive, more available, and strongly euphoric-producing substances (e.g., inhalants and hallucinogens). Other substances, it should be noted, are prevalent, and their high prevalence should not be overlooked. Although inhalants have seemingly become more available to more students, and more students have tried them since 1983, fewer students among those who have had an opportunity to try inhalants have tried such substances. The overall changes in prevalence levels between 1983 and 1988, however, may be interpreted as reflecting changes in patterns of use, and knowledge of these changes may help in furthering an understanding of students' experience with different mood-altering substances.

TABLE 5-2. Opportunity to Try and Trying Drugs Comparison: 1983-1988, Eight School Districts

Substance	1988[a] Percent	1983[b] Percent	Percent Change
Marijuana	75.9	74.8	+ 1.1
Cocaine	47.2	63.3	- 16.1[c]
Stimulants	66.0	76.2	- 10.2[c]
Hallucinogens	56.7	48.0	+ 8.7[c]
Depressants	51.4	71.6	- 20.2[c]
Heroin	26.5	29.9	- 3.4
Inhalants	57.3	61.5	- 4.2[c]
Tranquilizers	54.6	72.6	- 18.0[c]

[a]n=3814 [b]n=3609 [c]$p < .01$.

TABLE 5-3. Comparison of 1983 and 1988 Findings: Lifetime Experience with Chemical Substances, Eight School Districts

Substance	1988 Percent*	1983 Percent*	Percent Change
Marijuana	53.0	49.4	+ 4.0
Cocaine	14.4	18.3	- 3.9
Stimulants	24.2	27.2	- 3.0
Hallucinogens	13.2	8.7	+ 4.5
Depressants	9.8	14.3	- 4.5
Heroin	2.0	2.2	- 0.2
Inhalants	25.9	16.5	+ 9.4
Tranquilizers	9.9	11.5	- 1.6

*n=3814 **n=3609

4. Lifeuse Comparisons

Figure 5-1 shows a comparison of the overall number of students who tried one or more substances (excluding alcohol and tobacco) in 1983 and 1988. As observed, the number of students who tried a drug in 1988 increased by five percent. While there has thus been some decline in use of different substances, the increases that occurred for other substances were sufficiently large to contribute to an overall increase in lifetime experience with chemical substances. This increase, it should be noted, comes at a time when decreases in drug use have been reported across the nation (Bachman et al., 1988).

5. Number of Drugs Tried

Figure 5-2 shows a comparison of the number of drugs tried. More students tried one, two, or three drugs in 1988 than did students in 1983. In contrast, more students tended to try more than

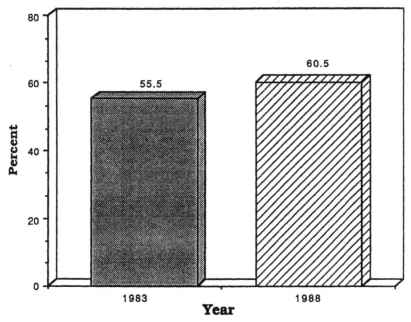

FIGURE 5-1. Comparison 1983 and 1988, Lifetime Experience

four substances in 1983 than in 1988. It may be that the current higher level of drug use, noted in Figure 5-1, is a function of greater experimentation with drugs than that which occurred previously. This hypothesis could be tested if a comparison of the frequency of drug use were possible, but because the questions were worded differently in the two surveys, a comparison of the frequency of drug use was precluded.

6. Lifetime Experience by Gender
Among Users

Figure 5-3 shows the proportion of male and female students who tried a drug based on all students who had ever tried a drug. The findings show that the proportion of male users increased slightly (1.1 percent) since 1983, while the proportion of female users decreased by a similar amount (1.1 percent). Males (52.0 percent)

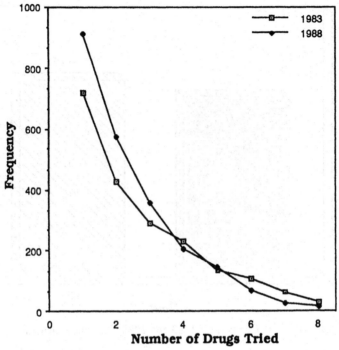

FIGURE 5-2. Number of Drugs Tried, 1983 and 1988

exceed females (48.0 percent) by 4 percent in the 1988 sample, while the margin of difference was 1.8 percent in 1983.

7. Lifetime Experience by Grade

Figures 5-4 and 5-5 report on the relationship between lifetime experience with a drug and grade level. The data indicate the percent of students who have tried one or more drugs during or before their current grade level.

Figure 5-4 represents the percent of students in each grade level *from among the entire sample* who reported ever having tried a drug. The data show a very different pattern for 1988 than for 1983. While the data from 1983 showed an increase from grades 7 to 9, the present findings showed a comparable number of students having tried drugs by grade seven, a greater increase in the number of

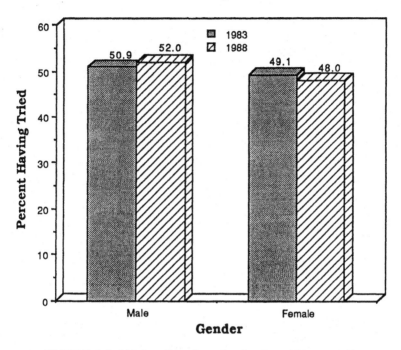

FIGURE 5-3. Lifetime Experience by Gender, 1983 and 1988

students who experience a drug by the 8th grade and, in contrast to 1983, a sharp decline in drug use among students in the 9th grade. Both samples show an increase in use for 10th grade students, but the 1988 sample shows a higher prevalence level. Use began to decline after the 10th grade in 1983, dropping sharply after the 11th grade. In the present sample, use declines very sharply in the 11th grade, but rises dramatically during the 12th grade.

When examining patterns of drug-taking behavior *within grade levels*, a different pattern emerges because of the nature of the analysis, which is based on a direct comparison of use and nonuse within each grade. Differences are also noted between 1983 and 1988 when a comparison is made among students *within each grade* level who tried drugs (Figure 5-5). While a corresponding increase in use and grade level is present for both samples, the increase for the 1988 sample is higher at the early grades (7-9) than later grades

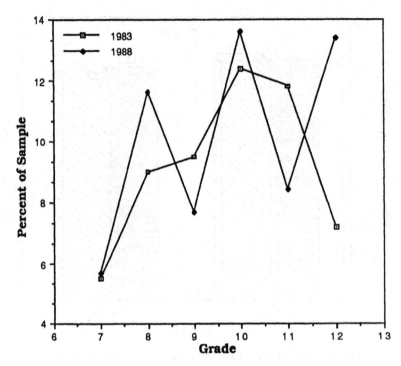

FIGURE 5-4. Lifetime Experience by Grade, 1983 and 1988

(11 & 12). Thus more students have experienced a drug at earlier grade levels in 1988 than in 1983, while fewer have tried drugs in the 11th and 12th grades in 1988 than in 1983.

8. Initiation into Drugs

The next series of figures compares the two studies' ages of initiation into drug use for each of the different substances.

a. Marijuana

Figure 5-6 illustrates initiation into marijuana. What is interesting to note is that both curves very generally approximate a normal distribution, with 13 years as the mode. In comparing the two distributions, fewer students were initiated into marijuana between 10 and 13 in 1988 than in 1983, but initiation declined for both groups

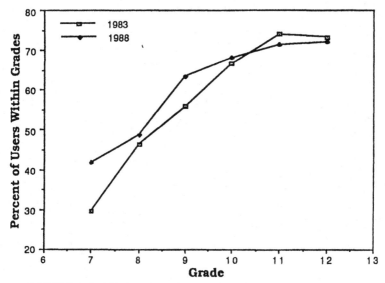

FIGURE 5-5. Lifetime Experience Within Grades, 1983 and 1988

after 13 years. Initiation was slightly higher at ages 14 and 15 for the present sample while initiation levels were comparable thereafter.

b. Cocaine

Initiation into cocaine shows a different pattern in 1988 than in 1983, as shown in Figure 5-7. Generally, initiation into cocaine for the 1983 sample shows increases until age 13, with a drop at age 14, then an increase at age 15, followed by a decline. Initiation into cocaine for the 1988 sample shows a steady increase beginning at age 10, which peaks at age 15, followed by a very slight decline; only after age 16 does initiation decrease. Initiation rates are higher at ages 14 and 17 for the current sample than for the 1983 sample.

c. Stimulants

Initiation into stimulant use shows a similar pattern (Figure 5-8), but with fewer students in the 1988 sample starting stimulant use after age 14 than in the 1983 sample.

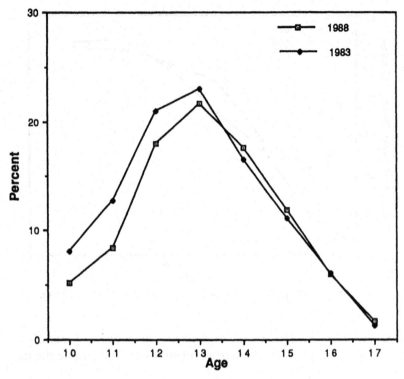

FIGURE 5-6. Initiation into Marijuana, 1983 and 1988

d. Hallucinogens

The two curves in Figure 5-9 show that fewer students have started hallucinogen use up to age 13 in the 1988 sample than in the 1983 group. But, after age 13, more students in the current sample started use at ages 14, 15, and 16.

e. Depressants

Initiation into depressants (Figure 5-10) shows a varied pattern between the two samples. There was a steady increase in initiation from ages 10 to 13 for both samples, but more students had tried within this age range in 1988 than 1983. Initiation into depressants

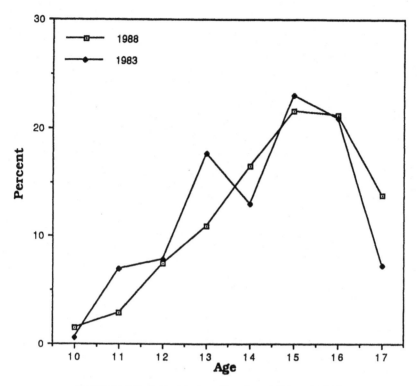

FIGURE 5-7. Initiation into Cocaine, 1983 and 1988

began to decline after age 13 for the 1988 sample, but not sharply until after age 15. In the 1983 sample initiation peaked at age 14, then declined sharply, but again showed a slight increase at age 16.

f. Inhalants

Except for a slightly higher initiation level at age 10 for the 1988 sample, the general pattern of initiation into inhalants, as shown in Figure 5-11, is similar. Initiation into inhalants appears to be highest between 12 and 13, and decreases thereafter.

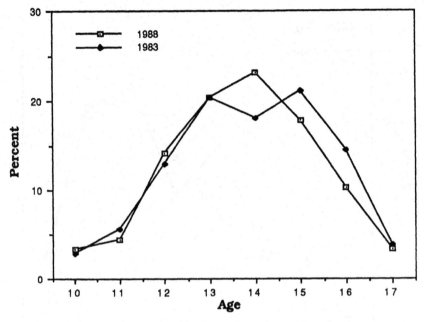

FIGURE 5-8. Initiation into Stimulants, 1983 and 1988

g. Tranquilizers

As shown in Figure 5-12, initiation into tranquilizers happened mainly between the ages of 10 and 14, but the 1988 sample, in contrast to the 1983 group, shows an extension of initiation until age 15, after which there is a sharp decline.

Figure 5-13 shows a comparison of the mean ages of initiation for each of the substances described above for 1983 and 1988. This figure permits a summary of the proceeding data. The plot of the means in Figure 5-13 helps to illustrate the changes in initiation that have occurred for each of the substances, based on the average age of initiation. A test of significance between the mean ages of initiation between 1983 and 1988 for each substance shows that the differences in age of initiation for marijuana (1983 mean = 12.92; 1988 mean = 12.58), stimulants (1983 mean = 13.90; 1988 mean

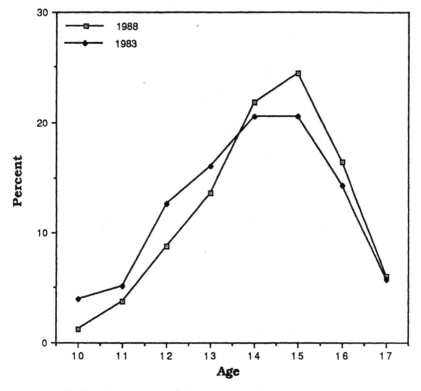

FIGURE 5-9. Initiation into Hallucinogens, 1983 and 1988

= 13.54), depressants (1983 mean = 13.69; 1988 mean = 13.02), and inhalants (1983 mean = 13.00; 1988 mean = 12.10), are statistically significant (p = < .01). There is thus a clear lowering of ages for initiation into these substances. Although cocaine and hallucinogens show an increase in age of initiation since 1983, the differences are not statistically significant.

Generally, the findings suggest that age of initiation covaries inversely with prevalence. Two of the three substances that show an increase in prevalence, marijuana and inhalants, also show a corresponding decrease in age of initiation. It may be that a self-regulation process has established itself among students who have tried drugs in the 1988 sample. That is, those substances that are readily

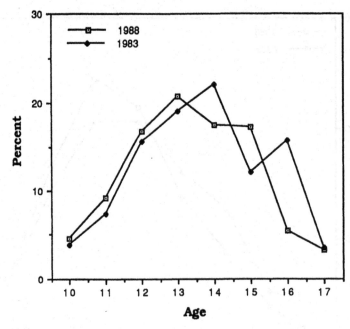

FIGURE 5-10. Initiation into Depressants, 1983 and 1988

available are tried much earlier, such as marijuana and inhalants, while other substances, which may be less available and which are considered to be "harder" drugs, are experienced later. This assumption, however, is in need of further study.

9. Alcohol

Figure 5-14 presents a comparison of prevalence levels for lifetime experience with alcohol for 1983 and 1988.[1] There is a slight increase (2.8 percent) observed for the 1988 sample.

---

1. Data for initiation into alcohol is unavailable for 1983, thereby precluding any comparisons on this variable.

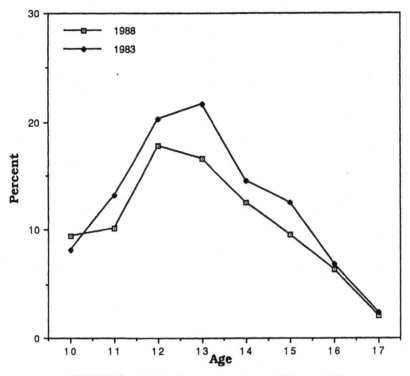

FIGURE 5-11. Initiation into Inhalants, 1983 and 1988

10. Smoking

Figure 5-15 shows there has been a 17 percent increase in life-time experience with cigarettes.

11. Age of Initiation of Cigarette Use

Figure 5-16, which compares age of initiation of smoking ciga-rettes for the two samples, shows that some changes have occurred. In 1988, fewer students were smoking at age 10 and 11 than in the 1983 sample, but more were beginning at age 12. After age 12 both samples show a steady decline, but more students tended to start

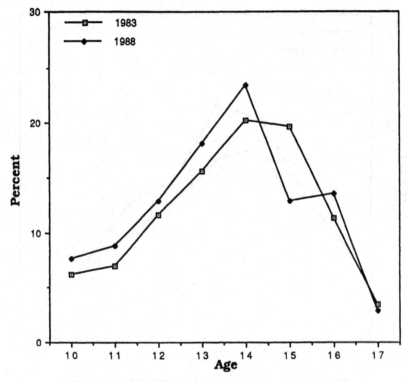

FIGURE 5-12. Initiation into Tranquilizers, 1983 and 1988

smoking at higher age levels in the 1988 sample than in the 1983 group.

B. DEMOGRAPHICS: REGIONAL COMPARISONS

The 1983 survey reported regional comparisons of drug-taking behavior. The regional groupings were based on sampling procedures followed in the 1983 study. The following three figures compare the 1988 findings with the 1983 results using the three regional groupings formed for the 1983 study.

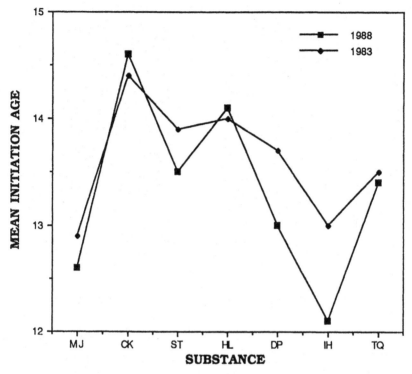

FIGURE 5-13. Mean Initiation Ages, 1983 and 1988

1. Anchorage-Barrow-Kotzebue-Nome-Sitka

A comparison of the 1983 and 1988 findings (Figure 5-17) shows considerable changes. Alcohol and tobacco, for example, have increased while experience with cocaine, stimulants, depressants and tranquilizers have decreased. Increases, however, are noted for marijuana, hallucinogens, and inhalants.

2. Bethel-Juneau-Fairbanks

The comparisons shown in Figure 5-18 also show variations since 1983. The largest increase is for smoking, with accompanying increases for lifetime experience with marijuana, hallucinogens, in-

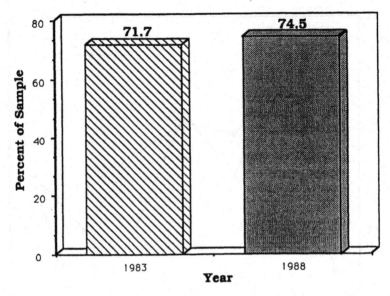

FIGURE 5-14. Lifetime Experience with Alcohol, 1983 and 1988

halants, tranquilizers, and alcohol. Decreases are observed for co-caine and depressants.

3. Barrow-Kotzebue-Nome

A pattern of change different from the preceding ones emerged in this region (Figure 5-19). While increases occurred for lifetime experience with marijuana, inhalants, alcohol, and tobacco, as noted in the other regions, decreases occurred for hallucinogens, cocaine, stimulants, depressants, and tranquilizers.

Based on these regional comparisons, it appears that there are certain patterns of drug-taking behavior both common and unique to the different regions of the state. For example, the different regions show a common trend with respect to increases in experiences with marijuana, inhalants, alcohol, and cigarettes, and a decrease for use of cocaine. Lifetime experience with the remaining substances, however, differs across regions in that some show increases while others decreased.

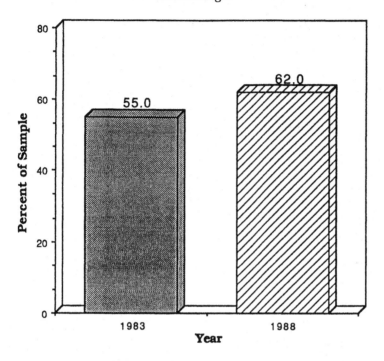

FIGURE 5-15. Lifetime Experience with Cigarettes, 1983 and 1988

SUMMARY

While the general level of drug-taking behavior stays fairly high within the state, there have nevertheless been changes in the pattern and prevalence of drug-taking behavior since 1983. Most prominent is the decline in experiences of substances except for marijuana, hallucinogens, and inhalants. Changes have also occurred with respect to age of initiation for the different substances. Marijuana, stimulants, depressants, inhalants, and tranquilizers have all shown a lowering of age in initiation, while the ages of initiation for cocaine and hallucinogens have risen. The patterns of changes within the regions suggest that while there is a general consistency across regions concerning use of some substances, there are also some patterns idiosyncratic to different locations.

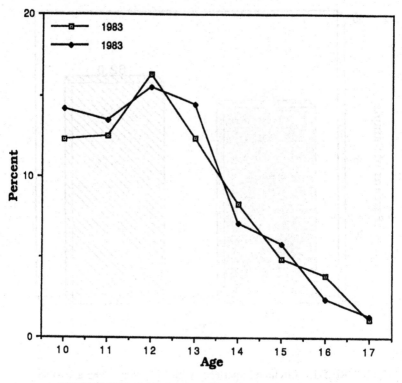

FIGURE 5-16. Initiation into Cigarettes, 1983 and 1988

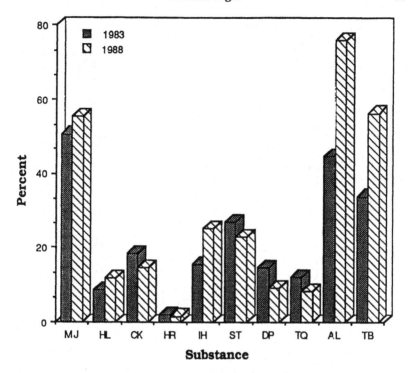

FIGURE 5-17. Comparison of Lifetime Experience: Anchorage-Barrow-Kotze-
bue-Nome-Sitka, 1983 and 1988

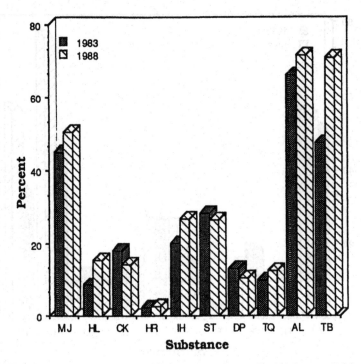

FIGURE 5-18. Comparison of Lifetime Experience: Bethel-Juneau-Fairbanks, 1983 and 1988

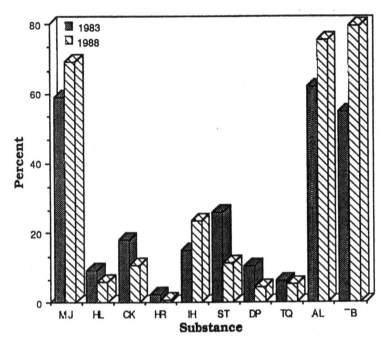

FIGURE 5-19. Comparison of Lifetime Experience: Barrow-Kotzebue-Nome, 1983 and 1988

Chapter 6

Comparisons:
Alaska and the Lower-48 States

The purpose of this chapter is to further an understanding of the prevalence of drug-taking behavior among adolescents by examining changes over time and variations among comparable age groups. A second aim is to determine the extent to which period or age effects are related to patterns of drug-taking behavior among adolescents. O'Malley, Bachman, and Johnston (1988) point out that there are three kinds of change that may occur in the prevalence of illicit and licit drug use: (1) period effects, which reflect changes with time, (2) age effects, which reflect developmental changes, and (3) cohort effects, which represent sustained or lasting differences among different graduating classes. The administration of two samples over time in Alaska, and a comparison of these findings with those from other research, provides an opportunity to account for variation in prevalence rates of various substances in terms of period or age effects.

A. COMPARISON WITH NATIONAL SURVEYS

1. Comparison of the Alaska 1983 and 1988
Eight-Community Samples with the National
Household Survey for 12-17 Year-Olds:
Lifetime Prevalence

Figure 6-1 compares the 1983 and 1988 Alaska Eight-Community findings for 12-17 year-olds with the 1982 and 1988 National Household Survey's (NIDA, 1989) findings for the same age group. The findings show clearly that Alaskan youth, as first ob-

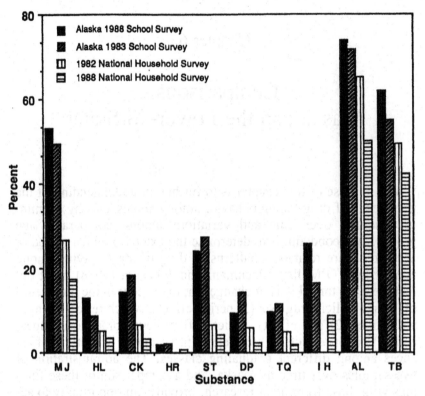

FIGURE 6-1. Comparison of Alaska School and National Household Surveys: 12-17 Year-Olds

served in 1983, continued to exceed their lower-48 counterparts in every category, and by considerable margins in many instances. Although there are variations in patterns of use on both the Alaska and National Samples, the change for some substances are in opposite directions. For example, the National Sample shows a decline in prevalence levels for marijuana, hallucinogens, alcohol and tobacco, while the Alaska data show increases in prevalence for these substances. Declines are noted in the 1988 sample, when compared to the 1983 findings, for cocaine, stimulants, depressants, and tranquilizers. Hallucinogens, however, show an increase.

These comparisons suggest that period effects may account for some of the differences that occurred concerning adolescent patterns of drug-taking behavior, but it is also important to note that regional or geographical differences may also contribute to the pattern of drug-taking behavior exhibited by youth. The differences, however, as noted in Figure 6-1, may be related more to the magnitude of use of different drugs than to differences in patterns of use. In Figure 6-1, for example, more Alaskan youth have tried the different substances, but the pattern of use is nevertheless fairly consistent for the different substances.

2. Comparison of 1988 Alaska Sample with the 1988 National Survey on Drug Abuse for 12-17 Year-Olds: Lifetime Prevalence

A comparison of the Alaskan data for the same age group (Figure 6-2) shows, as in Figure 6-1, that Alaskan 12-17 year-olds exceed the national levels for every substance.

3. Comparison of Alaska Seniors with the National High School Senior Survey: Lifetime Prevalence

Figure 6-3 provides a comparison of the 1983 and 1988 findings for Alaska high school seniors with the findings from the National High School Senior Survey (University of Michigan, 1989) for 1983 and 1988. Generally, the Alaskan data exceed national prevalence levels for both years. Also, as shown in the findings for 12-17 year-olds, Alaskan prevalence rates have tended to increase (e.g., inhalants and hallucinogens) while national rates increased or decreased, respectively. Conversely, a lowering of Alaskan prevalence levels for marijuana, cocaine and depressants are consistent with changes observed among national high school seniors.

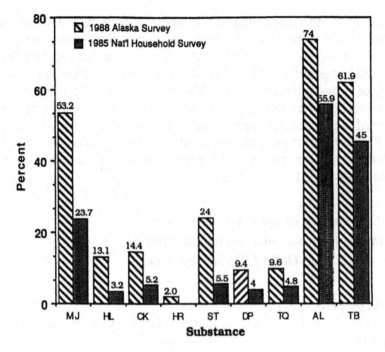

FIGURE 6-2. Comparison of Alaska and National Household Survey Findings for 12-17 Year-Olds: Total School Survey

B. COMPARISON WITH OTHER STATE SURVEYS

1. Lifetime Experience — Eighth Grade: Alaska, Oregon and Texas

Figure 6-4 provides a comparison of prevalence levels for drug-taking behavior reported for eighth graders in Oregon (Egan & Hallan, 1988) and Texas (Fredlund, Spence, & Maxwell, 1988) with eighth graders in Alaska. (Tranquilizers are not included in the Texas data.) The results of this comparison show that Alaskan eighth grades, overall, are not extremely different from their counterparts in two other lower-48 states. Alaskan youth, however, show higher prevalence levels for marijuana, stimulants, alcohol

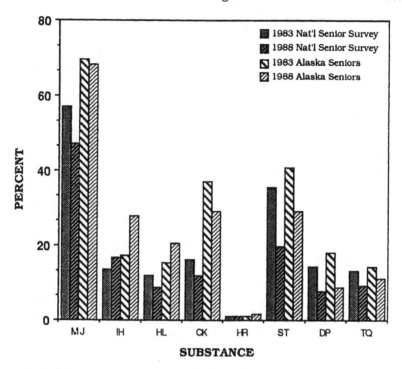

FIGURE 6-3. Comparison of High School Seniors: Alaska and National High School Surveys

and tobacco. Lower levels are observed for cocaine and heroin, with the remaining substances being at relatively comparable levels.

2. Eleventh Graders: Alaska, California, Oregon and Texas

Figure 6-5 compares 11th graders from four states. (Tranquilizers are not included in the Texas data.) Among these comparisons, Alaska's 11th graders show a prevalence pattern consistent with Alaska's eighth graders in that the 11th graders achieved the highest prevalence levels for marijuana, stimulants, alcohol, tranquilizers,

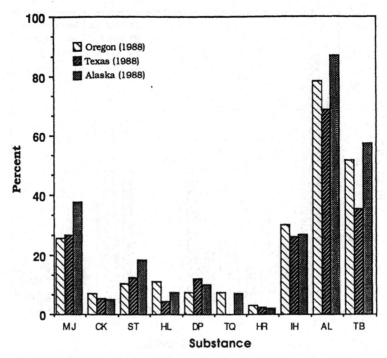

FIGURE 6-4. Eighth Grade Comparisons: Alaska, Oregon and Texas

and cocaine. Alaska is second to Oregon with respect to hallucinogens and inhalants, and is nearly equivalent to Oregon in the number of youth who reported having smoked. It should be noted that the California data (Skager et al. 1988) represent experience with a drug during the past six months, which may account for its generally lower prevalence levels. The data is included, however, to provide an additional comparison.

3. Past Month Use — Eighth Grade: Alaska, Oregon and Texas

When Alaska's eighth graders are compared to those in Oregon and Texas (Figure 6-6) concerning recency of experience (past month) with mood-altering drugs, Alaska's students show lower prevalence levels for all substances (except stimulants) than Oregon

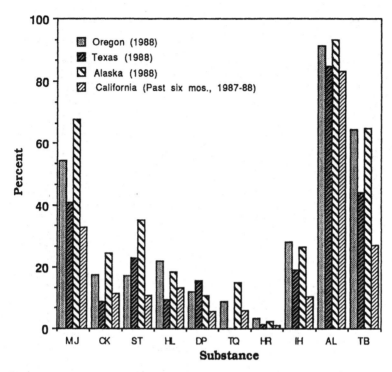

FIGURE 6-5. Eleventh Grade Comparisons: Alaska, California, Oregon and Texas

and Texas eighth graders. (Tranquilizer use was not assessed in the Texas survey.) These findings suggest that although Alaska may have an overall high prevalence level for lifetime experience with mood-altering substances, of those involved with drugs, eighth graders who have tried a substance have either experienced it and stopped, or may become very infrequent users after they first tried a substance. This conclusion, it needs to be noted, does not consider that the time of sampling may be a factor in the differences obtained. Nevertheless, they do point to possible regional differences for patterns of use. Alcohol and tobacco, however, are the exceptions since many students were either actively drinking or smoking during the past month in all three states.

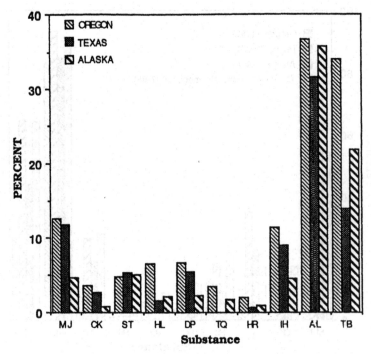

FIGURE 6-6. Past Month Experience—Eleventh Grade: Alaska, Oregon and Texas

4. Past Month Use—Eleventh Grade:
Alaska, Oregon and Texas

A comparison of 11th graders among the three states (Figure 6-7) on past month experience show that recency of experience, except for alcohol, is also lower in contrast to Oregon and Texas. (Tranquilizer use was not assessed in the Texas survey.) As with the eighth graders, prevalence for alcohol is high (the highest among the three states), along with tobacco and marijuana. The implications discussed for the eighth graders also pertain to the eleventh graders.

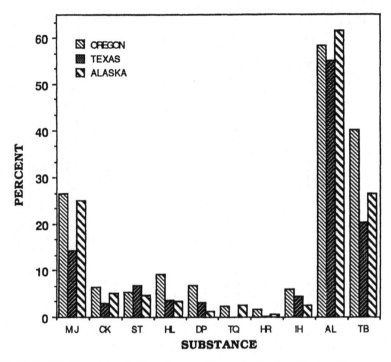

FIGURE 6-7. Past Month Experience—Eleventh Grade: Alaska, Oregon and Texas

5. Comparison of Alaska, California, Oregon and Texas with National Household Survey 12-17 Year-Olds: Ever Tried

Although the data in Figure 6-8 does not represent comparable samples, a general comparison of the findings from Alaska and Texas' studies of 7th to 12th graders, and California and Oregon's survey of 11th graders, was undertaken to explore how these findings matched those reported in the 1985 National Household Sample (NIDA, 1986). The California data represent having tried a drug during the past six months while the other data represent lifetime experience. The results of the comparison help to show where the four states stand in relation to national data.

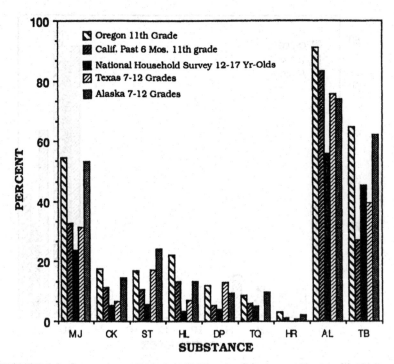

FIGURE 6-8. Comparison of Alaska, California, Oregon and Texas with National Household Sample 12-17 Year-Olds: Lifetime Experience and Past Six Months Experience

What this comparison shows is that all four states exceed the National Household Survey findings, except for tobacco, by considerable amounts. Because the California data is based only on past 6 month use, it can be assumed these figures would be higher if lifetime experience had been reported, approximating the prevalence levels in the other states. Alaska, however, while showing very high prevalence levels, these levels, which vary for specific substances, are not generally inconsistent with patterns of use found in the other states.

The question arises of why the data are so much higher among the four states than for the national survey. This is a particularly important finding because the nature of the differences suggests that the National data may underestimate drug-taking behavior among adolescents. One possible answer involves differences in method. The state surveys used a procedure which called for anonymous responses to questionnaires. The national study involved direct interviews and response to a written questionnaire in the respondent's home. It is possible that direct interviews, particularly when conducted in the interviewee's home, elicited more false negatives than responding anonymously to questionnaires in school, thereby resulting in lower prevalence rates. Another possible explanation is that regional findings which were not accounted for in the study, may be higher than the overall findings reported in the Household Survey for 12-17 year-olds. The factor of age may also contribute to some differences observed because eighteen-year olds or high school seniors were not included in the national data. This omission would tend to lower prevalence levels because seniors have generally shown high levels of drug use (Johnston et al., 1987, Segal, 1988). Period effects may also account for some of the differences observed. But, as Mensch and Kandel (1988) have found, the consistency of the lower national figures suggests that an underreporting of use of illicit drugs might have taken place because of interviewer effects.

In summary, the findings tend to support the O'Malley et al. (1988) notion that period and age effects contribute to changes that may happen over time to influence prevalence of drug-taking behavior. Other factors, however, need to be considered to provide a more complete account. One such factor appears to be a regional effect. For example, as trends develop in one section of the nation (e.g., California) they may, over time, expand to other locations (e.g., New York). However, immediately after a drug fad is incorporated into the lifestyle of those taking drugs in New York, a new trend may be started in California (cf. Skager & Fisher, 1985-1986). A cross-sectional study now would most probably show a greater prevalence in California than New York (i.e., a cultural lag) for a given substance.

Chapter 7

Discussion, Conclusions, Implications, and Recommendations

Communities throughout the United States have been particularly concerned with the problem of drug and alcohol use among youth for the past 25 years. This interest has been based on the belief that drug use can have catastrophic consequences for youngsters, who are both physically and emotionally immature, for their families, and for their communities. Based on this belief there has been a persistent struggle to understand the values and attitudes expressed by youth toward drugs, and to achieve perspectives on adolescent drug use patterns and trends. Developing an understanding of the problem "is an essential prerequisite for rational public debate and policy making" (Johnston et al., 1987, p. 4), both of which are crucial ingredients for planning countermeasures.

Alaska's geographical separation from the lower-48 states was thought to serve as a buffer to protect it from the drug-related problems that emerged in the 1960s. Alaska's physical separation, however, has not sheltered it from similar problems. Its youth are following, if not exceeding, the pattern of drug-taking behavior that is widespread among youth in the lower-48 states. In Alaska, as elsewhere, there is thus a need to monitor drug-taking behavior among youth to obtain reliable prevalence estimates. Without such information misconceptions can develop about the nature and scope of the problem, and early detection and localization of emerging problems become more difficult (Johnston et al., 1987).

The purpose of this research was to monitor drug-taking behavior among adolescents, specifically estimating prevalence and identifying trends. The following discussion integrates the study's findings into brief summary statements and ties them to the study's research aims. When proper, the implications of the findings are expounded.

1. To obtain information on the prevalence of specific chemical substances, including alcohol and tobacco.

Generally, the lifetime prevalence for experience with any chemical substances in Alaska is high. More adolescents within grades 7 to 12 (59.9 percent) have tried one or more substances than those not trying (40.1 percent). Prevalence rates are also high for lifetime experience with alcohol, cigarettes, and smokeless/chewing tobacco. The present findings show that prevalence levels are generally higher in 1988 than reported in 1983 (Segal, 1983), but individual variations took place with respect to use of different drugs.

2. To obtain demographic information about adolescents in grades 7-12 about use or nonuse of chemical substances.

The pattern of more male than female students trying drugs persisted, but what may be considered an important change in the relationship between grade level and drug use is observed. The 1988 data show a sharp decline in drug use among 9th and 11th graders, and higher prevalence levels in grades 8, 10, and 12, than found in the 1983 study. These changes cannot be attributable to differences in the number of students in the different grade levels of the current sample because the differences between weighted and unweighted prevalence levels within grades do not differ sharply (see Figure 4-7). Moreover, both the weighted and unweighted samples show a decline in prevalence for both the 9th and 11th grades. Related to this finding is an apparent change in initiation ages for different chemical substances; some, such as marijuana and inhalants, show earlier initiation ages while other substances, such as cocaine and hallucinogens, show increases in age of initiation.

What these findings suggest is that students seem to be varying their pattern of drug use, trying some substances earlier and delaying use of others until they are older. Mention was made earlier that a self-regulation process may be operating, in which students first try substances that are readily available and which are not perceived as "hard drugs," and then wait to try other substances such as cocaine and hallucinogens. Early research into the initiation of drugs by youth (Kandel, 1975) suggested a normative, orderly development sequence with drugs that is represented by four stages of adolescent involvement with drugs: (1) drinking beer and wine, (2) drinking distilled alcoholic beverages, possibly accompanied by smoking, (3) using marijuana, and (4) using other drugs. Based on the findings from the 1983 research, Segal (1986) reported that the sequence or patterns of first experience with different drugs changes over time. The present findings support this statement. Apparently, different peak years exist for trying different drugs, and that this pattern changes over time. This observation supports the notion of O'Malley et al. (1988) that period effects are related to changes in patterns of drug use that happen over time among adolescents.

Within the current sample, a higher percentage of students began smoking cigarettes at an age earlier (10 and 11) than beginning use of either marijuana or alcohol (see Figure 4-22). By age 12, however, initiation into smoking cigarettes peaks and then declines steadily while initiation into marijuana and alcohol show an identical initiation pattern, peaking at age 13, and then showing a steady decline. What may have happened since Kandel's (1975) report of what had occurred during the early 1970s regarding adolescent drug use, is that the four stages may have evolved into two: (1) smoking cigarettes, trying/using alcohol and marijuana, and (2) trying/using other drugs. Interestingly, research by Jones and Moberg (1988), who studied correlates of smokeless tobacco use among adolescent males, concluded that "smokeless tobacco use may be a new 'gateway' substance of abuse when age of first use is taken into account" (p. 62). Given the extensive use of smokeless tobacco within the present sample, and its early initiation (see Figure 4-21), along with cigarettes, both of which exceeded the number of students trying alcohol for the first time at ages 10 and 11, any understanding of longitudinal patterns of adolescent drug use needs to focus on the relationship between smoking and use of chewing or smokeless tobacco, and the function they serve as a pathway to experiences with alcohol and other substances.

It is possible to suggest, based on the current study, that marijuana and alcohol may be used interchangeably or simultaneously. This suggestion implies that marijuana has been accepted by a sig-

nificantly large number of youth because it may not be perceived as
particularly deviant or illicit, and that they may be interpreting or
perceiving its use in much the same way that the previous genera-
tion used alcohol. One of the implications of this conclusion involves the determination of what factors contribute to use of drugs
other than marijuana, and to identifying what factors are related to
initiation of tobacco products, drinking, and marijuana use. Effective reduction of use of these substances should contribute to reducing initiation into use of other illicit substances.

An examination of the relationship between ethnicity and drug-
taking (Figures 4-25 to 4-37) behavior among the total sample
shows that more Whites reported trying a drug or alcohol than any
other ethnic group. Alaska Natives show the second highest prevalence while prevalence levels among the remaining groups are not
essentially different.

A study of the proportion of youth *within* each of the different
ethnic groups (Table 4-26) shows that Alaska Native students show
the highest prevalence rate for ever having tried one or more drugs
(73.9 percent), followed by American Indians (72.6 percent). Hispanic students rank third (63.6), followed closely by students
grouped in the "Other" category (62.3 percent). Whites rank fifth
(57.2 percent), followed by Asian-Pacific students (51.3 percent),
and Blacks (41.1 percent). While the overall findings show that a
great many students placed emphasis on achieving an altered state
of consciousness provided by drugs, the findings report that drug
involvement within minority ethnic student groups is very high,
particularly for Alaska Natives, American Indians, Hispanics, and
students of mixed backgrounds (who are largely represented in the
"Other" category), a phenomenon that is consistent with findings
from other researchers (Gilbert, in press; Oetting & Beauvais,
1981, 1987; Segal, 1988; Skager, Fisher, & Maddehiam, 1986).

When an evaluation was made of the relationship between ethnicity and lifetime experience with each of the different substances,
including alcohol and tobacco products, the pattern which emerged
shows that Hispanic and American Indian youth achieve prevalence
levels which are disproportionately high with respect to their representation in the sample. Alaska Natives also show high prevalence

rates for use of chewing/smokeless tobacco and for having tried marijuana.

The above findings have important implications. One is that there is a clear need to begin to understand the broad array of social and cultural interactions regarding drug use within different cultural groups. While the behavioral and social norms regarding the use of a given drug may closely resemble each other in different ethnic groups, each cultural group may nevertheless ascribe different meanings, values and attitudes to drug use (Westermeyer, 1987). "In societies [such as Alaska, with its ethnic diversity], where ideal and behavioral norms differ with regard to the use of a particular drug, there is likely to be a widespread use of that drug, with all its associated problems" (Westermeyer, 1987, p. 21). Ethnographic studies can help to begin to provide critical information about how cultural attitudes, values, and behaviors interact concerning drug-taking behavior within different ethnic groups.

A second important implication is that concentrated efforts need to be directed at developing education and prevention programs that account for ethnic diversity and are responsive to the needs of a multicultural society. Prevention programs are usually concerned with changing attitudes about substance use (Simons, Conger, & Whitbeck, 1988). Such change, however, is largely successful among those youngsters who are most susceptible to such influences but do not impact youth who are most at risk for drug involvement (Oetting, Edwards, & Beauvais, 1988). If prevention efforts can be formulated to address the cultural factors within an ethnic group that place youngsters at high risk for drug involvement, then these efforts may be influential. For example, Oetting et al. (1988), state that

Drug involvement [among American Indian youth] is . . . primarily a function of peer clusters; dyads and small groups of close friends who mutually encourage drug use and who use drugs together. Underlying problems, such as poor family conditions and school adjustment difficulties, tend to increase the chances that an Indian child will make friends with other youth who also have problems, and the resulting peer clusters have a higher chance of getting involved with drugs. (p. 29)

Prevention efforts have to focus on changing those factors in the environment that contribute to and reinforce drug-taking behavior, instead of only concentrating on trying to change attitudes about using drugs.

The problem that Oetting et al. (1988) describes applies to all ethnic or cultural groups. The task is to identify and counteract the specific forces or influences within each ethnic group that are related to or influence drug-taking behavior. Such programs may need to start early in a child's development to be effective.

3. To obtain data about patterns of drug-taking behavior, including alcoholic beverages and tobacco products.

Several important findings relevant to patterns of drug-taking behavior emerge from this follow-up study. These are outlined below.

a. Overall Pattern of Use

There is both good and bad news for Alaska regarding drug-taking behavior from the present survey. The good news is that although the opportunity to try all illicit substances, except depressants, is reported to have increased, the number of students trying different substances when they had a chance to try it decreased for all drugs except marijuana and hallucinogens. Additionally, the lifetime prevalence has also decreased for all substances except marijuana, inhalants, and hallucinogens.

The bad news is that Alaska's lifetime prevalence for adolescent drug-taking behavior contrasts with national findings that reported a "downward trend in the use of *any illicit drugs*" [original emphasis] (Johnston et al., 1987, p. 15). Despite Alaska's decline in the use of some illicit drugs, Alaska's prevalence levels, except for lifetime experience with alcohol and depressants among high school seniors, exceed those reported in national surveys. Moreover, Alaska's lifetime prevalence levels generally exceed or match results from California, Oregon and Texas for comparably matched students. All four states, however, are higher than the results reported from the National Household Sample for 12-17 year-olds (see Figure 6-7). The fact that all four states are higher leads to the conclusion that the national study seems to have underreported prevalence level.

Concerning regional differences in Alaska, there are both common and unique prevalence levels within and across regions, but increases were noted for alcohol, marijuana, inhalants and hallucinogens across all regions of the state.

b. Marijuana

The prevalence rate for marijuana increased by (3.6 percent) in 1988, and is significantly different from the 1983 prevalence level. Marijuana is the illicit substance tried by most students, and the one used most frequently. It appears that marijuana use can no longer be considered a lifestage phenomenon, that is, an event that may be experienced by some youth at a time during adolescence because it is the "thing to do." The frequency with which marijuana was used in the current sample suggests that it is not an experimental event for many students, but that it seems to have become well incorporated into the lifestyle of many adolescents. Lifestyle is defined herein as a general term that implies that a drug (or drugs) has (have) become important to the individual. Newcomb and Bentler (1988a) have also noted that drug-taking behavior within their study group evolved into the lifestyle of teenagers. This pattern of use is in very sharp contrast with reports of a nationwide decline of marijuana among youth (Bachman et al., 1988).

The extensive use of marijuana by many adolescents in Alaska is a cause for concern because of the increasing research suggesting that marijuana may have adverse effects on physical health, particularly for developing adolescents.

One of the issues involved in the use of marijuana is whether its effects are subject to tolerance and physical dependence. The answer to this is an issue that remains open to interpretation. Some researchers strongly contend that tolerance develops, and that the onset is quite rapid (Nahas, 1979). Others indicate that "tolerance and withdrawal symptoms with marijuana do not develop" (Cohen, 1981). Blum (1984) states, "Carefully conducted studies with known doses of marijuana or THC leave little question that tolerance develops with prolonged use'' (p. 495). He continues to note that:

> The novice has a moderate degree of tolerance. With increasing exposure, tolerance appears to decrease, so that the occasional user has a low degree of tolerance and can smoke less to get the desired results. With increasingly heavy use, it rises again so a high degree of tolerance is developed and the user can smoke ten or more joints daily and get only mildly high. Withdrawal of the drug, especially in the chronic user, may evoke a psychic response because the individual feels the need for the drug and will seek it or some substitute. The anxiety, restlessness, insomnia, and other nonspecific symptoms of withdrawal are similar to those experienced by compulsive cigarette smokers. (p. 495)

The issue of whether one can develop tolerance to marijuana has not been completely resolved and studies continue. What is currently believed is that under conditions of heavy, sustained use, tolerance is manifested, but there is uncertainty about whether tolerance develops under conditions of low use.

There is also controversy over whether marijuana causes physical damage to the body, especially with long-term or chronic use. The research evidence suggests that some claims are substantiated while others are in need of more research. There is general agreement, however, that marijuana intoxication interferes with overall mental functioning, driving, psychomotor functioning, and learning. ''The effect on learning is pertinent, since much marijuana use occurs during school hours. The psychomotor deficits can last up to 4 to 10 hours after smoking, well beyond the duration of the 'high''' (Cohen, 1985, p. 62).

Another substantiated effect is on the respiratory system. Marijuana tars contain 50 percent more carcinogens than high-tar tobacco cigarettes, with 70 percent more benzopyrene in marijuana than in tobacco smoke (WHO, 1981). Using marijuana increases the risk of bronchial problems, such as sore throats, coughing, and susceptibility to bronchitis and pneumonia. The marijuana smoker is also subject to the risk of lung cancer and other disorders to which cigarette smokers are exposed, but the risk is higher because the smoke inhaled is unfiltered and has five to ten times the cancer-causing agents found in cigarettes. This risk is moderated, however, because marijuana smokers, in contrast to cigarette smokers, do not tend to chain smoke marijuana. Marijuana and tobacco users, however, run a risk of lung cancer that is higher than for use of either substance alone.

Other adverse physical effects that have been attributed to the use of marijuana are specific damage to the endocrine, immune, and reproductive systems; organic brain damage; and chromosome abnormalities. Research also suggests that marijuana may adversely impact the reproductive system of both males and females (Blum, 1984; Nahas, 1979). Frequent use of marijuana has been linked to a decrease in levels of serum testosterone, but it appears that the testosterone level may return to normal after smoking stops. There have been no reports, however, of abnormal offspring associated with marijuana use by the father (Blum, 1984). In females the use of marijuana is believed to affect the menstrual cycle, interfering with ovulation and lowering the period of fertility (Blum, 1984). In addition, because THC passes through the placental barrier, the risk of damage to the developing fetus is always possible. Marijuana use during pregnancy should be avoided. Moreover, if marijuana does adversely affect hormones related to sexual development as some believe (Nahas, 1979), its use may be especially harmful during adolescence, a period of rapid physical and sexual development.

Research studying whether marijuana causes chromosome abnormalities, endocrine disorders, and organic brain damage is being conducted, but results thus far have been inconclusive. There has also been a question of whether marijuana adversely affects the immunological system, but research results have been contradictory (Cohen, 1985) and the question has not been resolved.

It should be noted that any unsubstantiated claim that marijuana (or other drugs) causes physical damage (e.g., chromosome damage, impairment of the immunological system) may be counterproductive because such claims make marijuana users (and users of other drugs) skeptical about any negative statements about drugs, even if such reports are accurate and supported by research findings.

One effect that has been reported to be associated with chronic marijuana use is the "amotivational syndrome." The phrase was used by McGlothlin and West (1968) and Smith (1968) to describe a condition associated with regular marijuana use by youth in which the individual adopts an attitude and behavior that are asocial, non-directional, and a "cop-out" on established values. The amotivational syndrome is characterized by apathy, a loss of effectiveness, a diminished capacity to carry out complex, long-term plans, an inability to endure frustration and to concentrate for long periods, and an inability to follow routines or to master new material successfully.

There has been considerable controversy over whether the amotivational syndrome exists, and the debate continues. Cohen (1981) best summarized the issues concerning the amotivational syndrome as follows:

> What must be remembered is that large amounts of cannabis have a depressant effect upon the central nervous system, and equivalent amounts of alcohol or sedatives also would produce a decreased desire to work, poor performance, and a blunted emotional response. One difference is that THC is retained in the brain . . . for long periods because of its aqueous insolubility.
>
> Some young people do become sedated from considerable cannabis consumption. Others may become amotivated from discouragement about their situation, and marijuana ingestion simply reinforces their dropout from active participation in life. (pp. 37-38)

Because of the potential health risks associated with marijuana use for adolescents, the problem becomes one of developing an effective strategy to reduce and prevent its use.

The question arises of what factors may contribute to this high level of marijuana use in Alaska and elsewhere. Research (summarized in Bachman et al., 1988) has found that marijuana use is high when cigarette smoking, alcohol, and other illicit drugs are present. This is surely the case in Alaska, but is this circumstance enough to account for the high prevalence level? Probably not. Other factors have to be considered. One factor may be that Alaskan youth, despite the information conveyed about the adverse consequences of using marijuana, provide strong social support for using marijuana. Peer group support is a very powerful reinforcer for drug-taking behavior, and its importance cannot be overstated. (A discussion on peer group support, and a review of other factors contributing to use or nonuse of mood-altering substances, follows later.)

c. Cocaine

A positive finding is that cocaine use had declined, and that use of crack, a strong variant of cocaine, was low, but cocaine's overall prevalence level is high when compared to the findings from other research. The difference in prevalence levels between 1983 and 1988 are statistically significant. Initiation into cocaine, however, tended to be later than for other substances, but among those who tried it, a small proportion of students tended to use it with some degree of regularity.

d. Stimulants

A decrease in stimulant use is observed, a finding complementing that reported for the nation. The chief substances in this drug category are most probably amphetamines, a strong, euphoria-producing substance. The differences between 1983 and 1988 are statistically significant.

e. Hallucinogens

A statistically significant increase in hallucinogens is noted in 1988, with LSD most probably being the main hallucinogenic substance being tried. Anecdotal reports have indicated that it is currently available and is regaining popularity after a period of some decline.

f. Heroin

The prevalence level for heroin has been consistently low since 1983, and is generally consistent with reports from other research. (For more information about heroin in Alaska, see Fisher, Wilson, & Brause, in press.)

g. Depressants

Depressants, largely in the form of barbiturates, have experienced a decline since 1983, a trend that is consistent with reports from other surveys. The difference between the 1983 and 1988 prevalence levels is statistically significant.

h. Tranquilizers

Use of substances such as Valium or Librium, classified as tranquilizers, and used without a prescription, declined in 1988, and the current prevalence level is statistically different from the 1983 level, a trend which is consistent with findings from other research.

i. Inhalants

Of all the illicit chemical substances, inhalants have shown the largest increase, which is significantly different from the 1983 level. This increase is consistent with a small increase reported across the nation by Johnston et al. (1987). Inhalants have tended to be the substance of choice among very young users, largely because they are cheap, readily available, and induce an intense altered state of consciousness, maybe emulating the perceived experience of the substances the naive user cannot readily get. Also, older adolescents may resort to using inhalants when other substances are unavailable. Beauvais and Oetting (1987) noted that inhalant use, at every age, ·

> marks a very high level of drug involvement *for that group* and suggests potentially serious adjustment difficulties. Some of these difficulties include disruptive family relationships, poor school and job adjustment, serious emotional problems, and higher levels of deviance than other drug users. (p. 781)

The statistics regarding inhalants should be of particular concern because most, if not all inhalant substances, are highly toxic and can cause irreversible brain damage or death.

j. Alcohol

Consistent with the findings from different studies of drinking among youth across the nation, experience with alcohol in Alaska is ubiquitous among adolescents. It would also seem that drinking during adolescent years no longer represents a lifestage phenomenon, but has become an adolescent lifestyle phenomenon. Drinking among adolescents could be considered to model the drinking behavior of the adult population. Given that our society is persistently bombarded by advertising that espouses drinking, there is increasing concern that this advertising, while maybe not specifically targeted at adolescents, may nevertheless be influencing adolescents to drink (Orlandi, Lieberman, & Royce, 1988). Indeed, Atkin, Neuendorf, and McDermott (1983) have stated that "mass media advertising for alcohol plays a significant role in shaping young people's attitudes and behaviors regarding excessive or hazardous drinking" (p. 324). In contrast to Atkin et al.'s conclusion, Smart (1988), based on a review of the effects of advertising on alcohol consumption, indicates that the effects of advertising on drinking behavior are very small compared to other variables, such as availability and pricing. It seems clear that more needs to be known about the relationship between alcohol consumption, particularly among youth, and advertising, pricing, and availability. Additionally, further research is needed to understand the relationship between adult drinking patterns in the community and adolescent drinking patterns.

k. Tobacco

The prevalence of cigarette smoking and use of smokeless or chewing tobacco is alarmingly high in Alaska. Given the current attention to the harmful effects of smoking, it would be expected that adolescents would avoid tobacco products. To some extent, the unusually high use of smokeless or chewing tobacco might reflect an awareness among adolescents of the health risks of smoking and their turning to chewing or smokeless tobacco as a more desirable choice. The harmful effects of chewing or smokeless tobacco, however, have been well substantiated (Health Consequences, 1986). The use of tobacco products, as with alcohol, is also tied to commercial messages about smoking, with a particular emphasis on smokeless tobacco (McCarthy et al., 1986). It is therefore critical that further efforts be made to understand the role and function of smoking and use of chewing/smokeless tobacco among Alaska's youth, and to formulate strategies to reduce adolescent's use of tobacco products. This need is especially relevant for Alaska Native youth, who tend to show very high prevalence levels for use of chewing and smokeless tobacco.

4. To obtain information about some consequences of drug use.

One of the reasons for the intense concern over teenage drug use is the belief that it can have catastrophic consequences for the user, their families, and the community. Recent research, however, (Newcomb & Bentler 1988a, 1988b) suggested that "it is difficult to prove, in a causal sense, that teenage drug use created specific problems for young adults," (Newcomb & Bentler, 1988a, p. 64). Short-term consequences of acute substance use were noted, however, but varied with types of drugs used and dosage levels. The present research, however, did not explore the ramifications of drug-taking behavior in a substantive manner. Rather, only basic information was obtained on the consequences of drug use to derive a very preliminary understanding of the effects of drug-taking behavior.

A special cause for concern observed in the current finding was the observation that students reported drinking and driving. Evans (1987), following a comprehensive review of young drivers involved in automobile crashes, concluded that irresponsible driving has become a social norm among youth, which is tied to the way alcohol is portrayed to young drivers, particularly males. It is apparent that effective action needs to be taken to reduce drinking and driving among youthful drinkers, but most of the commonly proposed countermeasures, such as increasing the driver licensing age, and increasing the drinking age, have not been totally effective

(Evans, 1987). Recent research (cf., Lewis, 1988) has suggested that a single program directed at all youth may be less effective than developing programs that are carefully targeted according to age, subcultural group, and other characteristics of the recipients. Further research needs to be focused on understanding the impact on youth of the way in which driving is portrayed in comedy movies and television shows aimed specifically at young people. For example, how do young drivers respond to scene after scene in which they witness unbelted heroes or heroines have a major accident, jump out of the vehicle, unharmed and undaunted, to continue the chase by other means (Evans, 1987). Answers to this question may help to develop methods to establish safer social norms, without alcohol, for adolescent drivers.

One of the major questions resulting from this study is: Why do adolescents use drugs and alcohol? Although the present research did not focus on this question, an attempt to provide an answer is possible, derived from findings in the research literature. Segal (1985-86), based on findings from the 1983 study of Alaskan youth, reported three basic motives for drug use among adolescents which were consistent with other findings (Anglin, Thompson, & Fisher, 1986; Segal, 1983a; Segal, Huba, & Singer, 1980). The motives were described as follows:

1. *Tension reduction or coping*, which involves seeking the euphoric effects of drugs or alcohol to change consciousness to reduce or cope with stress, tension, or unpleasant or unwanted emotions.
2. *Drug effect*, which involves using drugs or alcohol to obtain an altered state of consciousness primarily to experience the drug's effect(s).
3. *Peer-related*, which involves using drugs chiefly in a social context, largely at the urging of friends, to enhance good times with friends (i.e., as a social lubricant).

Each of the above motives has implications for patterns of drug use. For example, students who use drugs primarily to reduce tension are at risk to progress from experimentation with drugs to abuse of drugs, and to use a variety of drugs to satisfy their needs.

Students who mostly experiment with drugs may limit their behavior to trying different substances a few times, but some of these students may be at risk to seek different and more intense experiences which may potentially lead to drug-related problems. Other students who try drugs as a function of peer pressure, and who start their drug use largely for social-recreational purposes, also share a potential for broadening their drug-taking behaviors and place themselves at risk for drug-related problems.

While each of these reasons for trying drugs may in and of itself serve as a primary motive to start drug-taking behavior, it is more probable that they interact, with each exerting a stronger influence at different times during an adolescent's development, and also vary in conjunction with the social context in which adolescents find themselves. It is probable that an interactive process is at work, reflecting a combination of several factors, each contributing a stronger effect at different times during an adolescent's personal and social development.

Johnston and O'Malley (1986) have reported very similar findings. They concluded that increased levels of drug use among adolescents was "both self-reflection of the more psychologically 'needy,' as well as the result of heavier users learning from their experience about the ends that can be achieved with a given drug" (p. 64). Johnston and O'Malley, as Segal (1985-86) before them, also noted that:

> One conclusion seems clear . . . many of the more frequent users . . . are using . . . substances for psychological coping — that is, to deal with negative affect, boredom, . . . and to gain more energy. (p. 64)

Binion et al. (1988) also reported that the most commonly-endorsed rationale for use of drugs involved the appeal of altered and pleasant sensations produced by the drugs, social facilitation, and the relief of negative affective states.

The above findings are helpful in forming an understanding of some *psychological* factors involved in drug-taking behavior. These factors which have shown themselves to be highly replicable across independent samples (Segal, 1985-1986), can be used to characterize subgroups of adolescent substance users based on their pattern of reasons for use. One could then develop different intervention and prevention strategies to address these different groups. For example, students identified as primarily social-recreational users (peer-related) might have a totally different characterization from those who are chiefly using drugs for self-medication (coping) or other self-enhancement motives, and both groups may differ from teenagers who try a drug just for experimentation (drug-effect) and then refrain from further use. In those cases where the coping motive prevails, intervention and prevention efforts need to be directed at changing attitudes that link the reduction of stress with altering one's state of consciousness. In the case where drug-taking behavior is largely tied to peer pressure, efforts to help adolescents overcome the negative influences of peers seem worthwhile. This effort should be increased when adolescents are at a high risk for initiation into drug-taking behavior rather than at a time which is more distant to initiation into drugs.

When motives for drug use center on the drug experience itself, efforts may need to be directed to introducing alternative behaviors that would simplify the achievement of "natural highs." This aim, however, has to be connected to a program that directs adolescent value systems away from attitudes held by many in our society who have come to accept drug-taking behavior as part of a lifestyle emphasizing the social and recreational use of drugs as a means of obtaining new and different experiences.

Helping adolescents to overcome the influences that peers exert on drug-taking behavior is another important task that needs to be advanced to help combat drug use among adolescents. Efforts have to be directed at understanding how or why some adolescents are more susceptible to social pressures than others, and to learn how to use this information to effectively intervene in initiation into drug-taking behavior.

Related to the problem of adolescent drug use is the question of identifying what factors distinguish nonusers from users (Anglin, Thompson, & Fisher, 1986; Segal, 1988), and what specific characteristics differentiate those adolescents who only experiment with drugs from those who become frequent users. Part of the answer involves the extent to which each of the motives described above exerts its influence singly, or in combination, with the others.

An important predisposition to the formation of these motives, however, is the environmental background that contributes to adolescents' attitudes and behaviors toward drugs and their use. It is almost without question that family use, and the child's involvement in the process of use by family members of alcohol and other drugs, is one of the most important influences related to the beliefs and values adolescents form about alcohol and other drugs. The contemporary emphasis on children of alcoholics within our country attests to the importance of understanding the relationship between heavy drinking by parents and the extremely damaging effect it has on children within the family. Along with drinking, an extremely strong relationship between teenage drug use and drug use by family members has also been shown (Anglin, Thompson, & Fisher, 1986; Fisher et al., 1987; Gfroerer, 1987; Kumpfer, 1987).

It should be noted that there are other important predisposing factors that contribute to adolescent drug-taking behavior that are intimately tied to the family. These are stressful life events encountered by youth early in life that interfere with successful adjustment during adolescence and adulthood. These events have been found to contribute to the need by some teenagers to use drugs to self-medicate a reduction in their level of stress. Youth at high risk for substance abuse have been found to have been either physically abused, sexually assaulted, or psychologically maltreated (Black, Bucky, & Wilder-Padilla, 1986; Dembo et al, 1988; Farber, 1987; Kroll et al., 1985; Sandberg, 1986). Such youngsters, despite whether they are male or female, tend to show evidence of depression, suicide, psychotic thinking, and aggressive behavior at some point in life, and alcohol and drug use may reach an extreme in their attempt to cope with their disorganized state.

The above discussion does not pertain to all adolescents who have experienced alcohol or other mood-altering substances, but it may help explain why some start drug-taking behavior earlier than others, use more illicit drugs or drink alcohol more frequently, and encounter greater difficulty resulting from their drug-taking behavior.

It also needs to be noted that not only parents, but peers can have a strong influence on adolescent drug-taking behavior, the degree of influence for each varying at different ages and stages of development. Kandel (1986) has pointed out that peer influences predominate on current life-style influences, while parental influences are especially strong on basic values and future life goals and aspirations.

A recent report by Oetting and Beauvais (1987) may help to provide a perspective on peer influence on drug-taking behavior that is particularly relevant to Alaska. Their concept of "peer cluster theory" contends that "peer clusters shape and determine the attitudes, values, and beliefs about drugs . . . and, to a great extent, determine the actual drug-taking behaviors—what drugs are used and when, where, and how they are used" (p. 206). A peer group is a group with which a youth is associated. A *peer cluster* is a very small subset of peers that closely share attitudes, values, and beliefs. Given the geographical isolation of Alaskan communities, especially those accessible only by air, peer cluster theory becomes an interesting concept that can help to explain why Alaska's prevalence levels are so high.

In the context of the theory, peer clusters are likely to use the same drugs, use them for the same reasons and use them together. Given the geographical isolation within Alaska, it seems that young people with similar attitudes toward drugs would seek each other's company and would thus tend to reinforce each other's drug-taking behavior. Oetting and Beauvais (1987) have found a significantly strong relationship between a youth's drug use and his or her association with peers who encourage drug use.

Another important aspect involved in trying to develop an understanding of adolescent drug-taking behavior is the issue of whether such behavior is deviant. There is one orientation that has generally viewed any form of drug-taking behavior by youth as bad or deviant (Donovan & Jessor, 1985; Jessor & Jessor, 1977; Kandel, 1975; Kandel et al., 1978; Kaplan et al., 1982; Osgood, 1985; Smith & Fogg, 1978, 1980). A contrasting view has been advanced by other researchers who interpret experimental or limited social or recreational use of drugs as not necessarily deviant (Huba et al., 1979, 1980; Newcomb & Bentler, 1988b; Segal et al, 1980; Thompson et al., 1985). Rather, such behavior is perceived as more of a function of behavioral styles that interrelates with interpersonal and socio-cultural factors. In this context those who are more likely to try drugs would also show higher levels of *rebelliousness, autonomy strivings, liberalism,* and a *willingness to try new experiences,* when compared to their nonusing counterparts (Segal, 1988).

The characteristic of rebelliousness does not include defiance or alienation as part of its definition. Instead, rebelliousness represents a breaking away from conformity and an indifference to social consciousness or to presenting oneself in a favorable light. There is a flouting of or contempt for rules and regulations, which may, in large part, seek its expression in drug-taking behavior.

Autonomy strivings represent an attempt to break away from constraints or restrictions, such as parental and societal controls. There is an enjoyment of being unattached, free, and without any obligations. These needs for autonomy and rebelliousness are highly interrelated; if autonomy strivings are experienced as being frustrated, then rebelliousness may intensify and include defiance and an overt contempt for conformity.

Liberalism represents an openness to new ideas and knowledge, together with policies that allow freedom for individuals to act or express themselves as they choose. Use of drugs is interpreted as a right of personal choice instead of as deviant behavior.

The wish for new experiences characterizes those who might experiment with drugs, or use them with some degree of regularity, as part of a tendency to seek out new and different, exciting or stimulating experiences; the psychoactive properties of drugs readily provide such stimulation (Segal, 1988; Thompson et al., 1985).

It should be noted that the characteristics described are very general, and apply to those involved in nonproblem, limited recreational or experimental drug-taking behavior. These personality characteristics, when grouped together, are attributes that tend to reflect a general lifestyle that seems to prevail among many of those who try to use drugs. Involved in this lifestyle is a tendency to seek out new experiences and a willingness to try high-risk activities, including taking drugs. It does not appear that there is any implication that "deviance" accounts for the strong relationship between what may be called "sensation seeking" and drug-taking behavior (c.f., Anglin et al., 1986; Bates et al., 1986; Margot, 1986; Segal,

1988; Zuckerman, 1983). Instead, it appears that initiation into drug-taking behavior, particularly for youth, may be best understood as a means of fulfilling a need to undergo new experiences, even if it involves unconventional behavior. Such behavior, it should be noted, is far removed from the traditional problems of narcotic dependence and other forms of drug-related problems. With pervasive use of drugs, however, the probability of associated "deviance" increases greatly; that is, using drugs may begin to serve needs other than just seeking stimulation as part of one's lifestyle.

With respect to what all the above means for prevention of drug-taking behavior, it is apparent that any attack on adolescent drug use *cannot* focus on the drug alone. Prevention efforts must include dealing with problems resulting from family disruptions, personal problems, and peer influences, as well as efforts to reduce the availability of drugs. Effective prevention may be achieved only by dealing with the various factors that promote drug-taking behavior. Only a comprehensive educational program that considers most of the factors that affect the target population may prove to be effective. School-based prevention programs that focus on a single factor may be beneficial for some adolescents and destructive for others (Kirschenbaum, 1983). Contemporary prevention efforts have to begin to focus on health promotion and health protection as a primary way of preventing drug use. One of the ways in which prevention efforts can be more successful is to help students sever the perceptual link between drug use and coping behavior and drug use and mood change, and to foster new behaviors that provide *more desirable* and *more rewarding choices* than using drugs. The major task that lies ahead is to formulate strategies or procedures that will help to break this perceptual link.

An important issue which is of considerable concern in Alaska is: what is the relationship between Alaska's decriminalization of marijuana and its apparent high prevalence in the state? There is no easy answer to this question. Any attempt to assess the impact of decriminalization is fraught with difficulty. It is hard to determine the consequences of the legal change. For example, if marijuana use has increased, is this increase a function of greater recognition of the problem because of a greater emphasis on law enforcement, or a function of increased use because of less severe penalties? Depending on one's views, several contrasting conclusions can be made about decriminalization: (1) decriminalization has had little or no effect on patterns and extent of marijuana use, (2) that marijuana use has significantly increased following decriminalization, or (3) that the social problem caused by marijuana abuse, at least as reflected in law enforcement costs, has decreased following legal change.

There is also the very real possibility that it is not the legal change that is most significant, but rather a whole set of other factors that may interact with decriminalization to contribute to the level of drug use in the state. Changes in patterns of law enforcement, drug availability, age of users, and self-perceived benefits or risks, all combine to form a complex interaction which may have no effect or very direct consequences on the prevalence of marijuana use.

Another concern of the research is the validity of the self-reports of the students. The validity of self-reports is always questioned, particularly when the self-reports concern a sensitive topic such as drug use. Although every effort has been made to get reliable and valid results (see Chapter 3), it is not known to what extent students who reported having tried a drug actually experienced the substance, that is, whether they used the real drug as opposed to a look-alike or a substitute substance. The important fact, however, is that the students apparently believed that they took the substance, and reported its use. The extent to which students who used a drug and did not report its use (false negative) is not known. Nor is it possible to determine the extent to which students who did not use a drug indicated that they did use it (false positives).

The data, however, are remarkably consistent across districts, and generally consistent with the 1983 findings, suggesting that reliable and valid results have been obtained. With the proliferation of survey research over the past 15 years, concern over the accuracy of self-reports by adolescents has shown that such reports are valid (Campanelli, Dielman, & Shope, 1987).

In conclusion, it is important to note that the recent history of attempts to deal with the problem of drug abuse through strong legislation aimed at punishing the user and penalizing distributors has not worked in the United States. Such efforts have resulted in a preoccupation with punishment, which has not resulted in a general reduction of drug use. It has been shown that punitive approaches place an unfair and sometimes overwhelming burden on the justice system, leading to an unrealistic expectation that law enforcement agencies will stop the problem (Joint Committee on New York Drug Law Evaluation, 1978). Energy needs to be directed instead toward focusing on youth and on the circumstances that contribute to their use of drugs, as well as on reducing the availability of drugs.

What is needed is an integrated approach that brings together representatives from the legal, social, and health professions, law enforcement, educators, legislators, and governmental authorities, to pool their resources, experience, and knowledge to develop a rational and comprehensive public policy aimed at reducing the problem of drug and alcohol abuse. Accomplishing this goal, however, requires that an investment of money be made to support the implementation of public policy procedures directed at reducing alcohol and drug abuse.

List of References

Analysis of Sex Offender Data. (1985). Juneau, AK: Department of Corrections.

Anglin, D. M., Thompson, J. P., & Fisher, D. G. (1986). Parental, personality, and peer correlates of psychoactive mushroom use. *Journal of Drug Education, 16*(3), 265-285.

Atkin, C. K., Neuendorf, K., & McDermott, S. (1983). The role of alcohol advertising in excessive and hazardous drinking. *Journal of Drug Education, 13,* 313-325.

Bachman, J. G., Johnston, L. D., O'Malley, P. M., & Humphrey, R. H. (1988). Explaining the recent decline in marijuana use: Differentiating the effects of perceived risks, disapproval, and general lifestyle factors. *Journal of Health and Social Behavior, 29,* 92-112.

Bates, M.E., Labouvie, E. W., & White-Raskin, H. (1986). The effects of sensation seeking needs on alcohol and marijuana use in adolescents. *Bulletin of the Society of Psychologists in Addiction Studies, 5,* 29-36.

Beauvais, F., & Oetting, E. R. (1988). Toward a clear definition of inhalant abuse. *The International Journal of the Addictions, 22*(8), 779-784.

Binion, A. Jr., Miller, C. D., Beauvais, F., & Oetting, E. R. (1988). Rationales for the use of alcohol, marijuana, and other drugs by eighth-grade Native American and Anglo youth. *The International Journal of the Addictions, 23*(1), 47-64.

Black, C., Bucky, S. F., & Wilder-Padilla, S. (1986). The interpersonal and emotional consequences of being an adult child of an alcoholic. *The International Journal of the Addictions, 21*(2), 213-231.

Blum, K. (1984). *Handbook of abusable drugs.* New York: Gardner Press.

Campanelli, P. C., Dielman, T. E., & Shope, J. T. (1987). Validity of adolescents' self-reports of alcohol use and misuse using a bogus pipeline procedure. *Adolescence, XXXII*(85), 7-22.

Cisin, I., Miller, J., & Harrell, A. V. (1988). *Highlights from the National Survey on Drug Abuse: 1977.* Washington, DC: Superintendent of Documents, U.S. Government Printing Office.

Cohen, S. (1981). *The substance abuse problem.* New York: The Haworth Press.

Cohen, S. (1985). *The substance abuse problems. Volume Two: New Issues for the 1980s.* New York: The Haworth Press.

Dembo, R., Dertke, M., Borders, S., Washburn, M., & Schmeidler, J. (1988). The relationship between physical and sexual abuse and tobacco, alcohol, and illicit drug use among youths in a juvenile detention center. *The International Journal of the Addictions, 23*(4), 351-378.

Department of Health and Social Services. (1983). *Annual report to the Legislature 1982.* Juneau, AK: Department of Health and Social Services.

Department of Public Safety. (1988). *Alaska State Troopers, Drug report to the Alaska Legislature, January 1, 1986-June 30, 1987.* Juneau, AK: Department of Public Safety.

Donovan, J. E., & Jessor, R. (1985). Structure of problem behavior in adolescence and young adulthood. *Journal of Consulting and Clinical Psychology, 53*, 890-904.

Egan, D. M. & Hallan, J. B. (1988). *Drug use by Oregon public school students.* Portland, OR: Office of Alcohol and Drug Programs, Oregon Department of Human Resources.

Evans, L. (1987). Young drivers involvement in severe car crashes. *Alcohol, Drugs and Driving, 3*(3-4), 45-62.

Farber, E. D. (1987). The adolescent who runs. In B. S. Brown & A. R. Mills (Eds.), *Youth at risk for substance abuse* (pp. 158-168). Rockville, MD: National Institute on Drug Abuse.

Fisher, D. G., Wilson, P. J., & Brause, J. (In Press). Intravenous drug use in Alaska. *Drugs & Society: A Journal of Contemporary Issues.*

Fisher, D. G., MacKinnon, D. P., Anglin, M. D., & Thompson, J. P. (1987). Parental influences on substance use: Gender differences and stage theory. *Journal of Drug Education, 17*(1), 69-85.

Fredlund, E. V., Spence, R. T., & Maxwell, J. C. (1989). *Substance use among students in Texas secondary schools–1988*. Austin, TX: Texas Commission on Alcohol and Drug Use.

Gilbert, M. J. (1988). Alcohol use among Latino Adolescents: What we know and what we need to know. *Drugs and Society*, *3*(1/2), 35-54.

Gfroerer, J. (1987). Correlation between drug use by teenagers and drug use by older family members. *American Journal of Drug and Alcohol Abuse*, *12*(1 & 2), 95-108.

Huba, G. J., Wingard, J. A., & Bentler, P. M. (1979). Adolescent drug use and peer and adult interaction patterns. *Journal of Consulting and Clinical Psychology*, *47*, 265-276.

The Health Consequences of Using Smokeless Tobacco. (1986). Public Health Service. Washington, DC: U.S. Department of Health and Human Services.

Jessor, R. J., & Jessor, S. (1977). *Problem behavior and psychological development*. New York: Academic Press.

Johnston, L. (1983). *Drugs and American youth*. Ann Arbor, MI: Institute for Social Research.

Johnston, L. (1988). *Selected tables from The 1987 National High School Senior Survey*. Ann Arbor, MI: The University of Michigan.

Johnston, L., & O'Malley, P. M. (1986). Why do the nation's students use drugs and alcohol? Self-reported reasons from nine national surveys. *The Journal of Drug Issues*, *16*(1), 29-66.

Johnston, L. D., O'Malley, P. M., & Bachman, J. G. (1987). *National trends in drug use and related factors among American high school students and young adults, 1975-1986*. Rockville, MD: National Institute on Drug Abuse.

Joint Committee on New York Drug Law Evaluation. (1978). *The nation's toughest drug law: Evaluating the New York experience*. Washington, DC: Law Enforcement Assistance Administration.

Jones, R. B., & Moberg, D. P. (1988). Correlates of smokeless tobacco use in a male adolescent population. *The American Journal of Public Health*, *78*(1), 61-63.

Kandel, D. B. (1975). Stages in adolescent involvement in drug use. *Science*, *190*, 912-914.

Kandel, D. B. (1986). Processes of peer influence in adolescence.

In R. K. Silbereisen (Ed.), *Development as action in context.* Berlin: Springer-Verlag.

Kandel, D. B., Kessler, R. C., & Margulies, R. Z. (1978). Antecedents of adolescent initiation into stages of drug use: A developmental analysis. In D. B. Kandel (Ed.), *Longitudinal research on drug use: Empirical findings and methodological issues* (pp. 73-100). Washington, DC: Hemisphere.

Kaplan, H. B., Martin, S. S., & Robbins, C. (1982). Application of a general theory of deviant behavior: Self-derogation and adolescent drug use. *Journal of Health and Social Behavior, 23,* 274-294.

Kirschenbaum, D. (1983). Toward more behavioral early intervention programs: A rationale. *Professional Psychology: Research & Practice, 14,* 159-169.

Kroll, P. D., Stock, D. F., & James, M. E. (1985). The behavior of adult alcoholic men abused as children. *The Journal of Nervous and Mental Disease, 173*(11), 689-693.

Kumfer, K. L. (1987). Special populations; Etiology and prevention of vulnerability to chemical dependency in children of substance abusers. In B. S. Brown & A. R. Mills (Eds.), *Youth at risk for substance abuse* (pp. 1-72). Rockville, MD: National Institute on Drug Abuse.

Lewis, C. (1988). Preventing traffic casualities among youth: What is our knowledge base? *Alcohol, Drugs and Driving, 4*(1), 1-8.

Lonner, T. D. (1983). *Major construction projects and changing substance use patterns in Alaska.* Anchorage, AK: The Center for Alcohol and Addiction Studies, University of Alaska, Anchorage.

McCarthy, W. J., Newcomb, J. D., Maddahian, E., & Skager, R. (1986). Smokeless tobacco use among adolescents: Demographic differences, other substance use, and psychological correlates. *Journal of Drug Education, 169*(4), 383-402.

McGlothlin, W., & West, L. J. (1968). The marijuana problem: An overview. *American Journal of Psychiatry, 125,* 1126-1134.

Marget, S. R. (1986). The relationship between frequency of marijuana use and reasons for marijuana use in college students. Unpublished Master's Thesis, Northern Arizona University, Flagstaff.

Mensch, B. S., & Kandel, D. B. (1988). Underreporting of substance use in a national longitudinal youth cohort; Individual and interviewer effects. *Public Opinion Quarterly*, *52*, 100-124.

Millstein, S. G., & Irwin, C. E. Jr. (1988). Accident-related behaviors in adolescents: A biopsychosocial view. *Alcohol, Drugs and Driving*, *4*(1), 21-30.

Moskowitz, H. (Ed.). Youth at risk for traffic accidents. Proceedings of an international symposium held in Santa Monica, California, May 29-31, 1987. *Alcohol, Drugs and Driving*, *3*(3-4) (Whole issue).

Moskowitz, H. (Ed.). Youth at risk for traffic accidents. Proceedings of an international symposium held in Santa Monica, California, May 29-31, 1987. Part II. *Alcohol, Drugs and Driving*, *4*(1) (Whole Issue).

Moser, C., & Kalton, G. (1971). *Survey methods in social intervention*. London: Heinemann Educational Books.

Nahas, G. (1979). *Keep off the grass*. New York: Pergamon.

National Institute on Drug Abuse. (1989). National Household Survey on Drug Abuse, 1988. *NIDA Capsules*.

Newcomb, M. D., & Bentler, P. M. (1988a). Impact of adolescent drug use and social support on problems of young adults: A longitudinal study. *Journal of Abnormal Psychology*, *97*(1), 64-75.

Newcomb, M. D., & Bentler, P. M. (1988b). *Consequences of adolescent drug use. Impact on the lives of young adults*. Newbury Park, CA: Sage Publications.

Oetting, E. R., & Beauvais, F. (1981). *Drug use among Native-American youth: Summary of findings (1975-1981)*. Fort Collins, CO: Colorado State University.

Oetting, E. R., & Beauvais, F. (1987). Peer cluster theory, socialization characteristics, and adolescent drug use: A path analysis. *Journal of Counseling Psychology*, *34*(2), 205-213.

Oetting, E. R., Edwards, R. W., & Beauvais, F. (1988). Drugs and Native-American youth. In B. Segal (Ed.), *Drugs & Society*, *3*(1/2), 1-34.

O'Malley, P. M., Bachman, J. G., & Johnston, L. D. (1988). Period, age, and cohort effects on substance use among young Americans: A decade of change: 1976-86. *American Journal of Public Health*, *78*(10), 1315-1231.

Orlandi, M. A., Lieberman, L. R., & Royce, J. (1988). The effects of alcohol and tobacco advertising on adolescents. *Drugs & Society, 3*(1/2), 77-98.

Osgood, D. W. (1985). *The drug-crime connection and the generality and stability of deviance*. Paper presented at the meeting of the American Society of Criminology.

Persily, L. (1989, March, 23). Senate OKs pot penalties. *Anchorage Daily News*, pp. C1, 3.

Poppe, R. L. (1973). *Pipeline impact on drug use & abuse to the Socio-economic Impact Committee on the Pipeline Impact Study*. Juneau, AK: Office of Drug Abuse. (Memorandum)

Porter, M. R., Vieira, T. A., Kaplan, G. J., Heesch, J. R., & Colyar, A. B. (1973). Drug use in Anchorage, Alaska. *Journal of the American Medical Association, 223*, 657-664.

Richards, L. G. (1981). *Demographic trends and drug abuse 1980-1995*. (research Monograph Series 35). Rockville, MD: National Institute on Drug Abuse.

Sandberg, D. N. (1986). The child abuse-delinquency connection: Evolution of a therapeutic community. *Journal of Psychoactive Drugs, 18*(3), 215-220.

Segal, B. (1983a). *Patterns of drug use: Report of a statewide school survey*. Juneau, AK: Department of Health and Social Services.

Segal, B. (1983b). *Patterns of drug use: Report of a statewide community survey*. Juneau, AK: Department of Health and Social Services.

Segal, B. (1985-86). Confirmatory analyses of reasons for experiencing psychoactive drugs during adolescence. *The International Journal of the Addictions, 20*(11 & 12), 1649-1662.

Segal, B. (1986). Age and first experience with psychoactive drugs. *The International Journal of the Addictions, 21*(12), 1285-1306.

Segal, B. (1988). *Drugs and society: Cause, effects, and prevention*. New York: Gardner Press.

Segal, B., Huba, G. J., & Singer, J. L. (1980). *Drugs, daydreaming and personality: A study of college youth*. Hillsdale, NJ: Erlbaum.

Selltiz, C., Jahoda, M., Deutsch, M., & Cook, S. (1967). *Re-*

search methods in social relations. New York: Holt Rinehart and Winston.

Simons, R. L., Conger, R. D., & Whitbeck, L. B. (1988). A multistage social learning model of the influences of family and peers upon adolescent substance abuse. *Journal of Drug Issues, 18*(3), 296-316.

Simpson, H., & Mayhew, D. R. (1987). Demographic trends and traffic casualties among youth. *Alcohol, Drugs and Driving, 3*(3-4), 45-62.

Skager, R., & Fisher, D. (1985-1986, Winter). *Drug and alcohol use among California eleventh grade students in relation to school characteristics*. Sacramento, CA: Office of the Attorney General.

Skager, R., Fisher, D., & Maddahian, E. (1986). *A statewide survey of drug and alcohol use among California students in grades 7, 9, and 11*. Sacramento, CA: Office of the Attorney General.

Skager, R., Frith, S. L., & Maddahian, E. (1988). *Second statewide survey of drugs and alcohol use among California students in grades 7, 9, and 11*. Los Angeles, CA: University of California, Los Angeles.

Smart, R. G., (1988). Does alcohol advertising affect overall consumption? A review of empirical studies. *Journal of Studies on Alcohol, 49*(4), 314-323.

Smith, D. E. (1968). *Powers of the mind*. New York: Ballantine.

Smith, G. M., & Fogg, C. P. (1978). Psychological predictors of early use, late use, and nonuse of marijuana among teenage students. In D. B. Kandel (Ed.), *Longitudinal research on drug use: Empirical findings and methodological issues* (pp. 101-113). Washington, DC: Hemisphere.

Smith, G. M., & Fogg, C. P. (1980). Psychological antecedents of teenage drug use. In R. Simmons (Ed.), *Research in community and mental health: An annual compilation of research* (Vol. I). Greenwich, CT: JAI.

SPSS-X User's Guide (3rd Edition). Chicago, IL: SPSS Inc.

State Office of Drug Abuse. (1975). *Alaska state plan for drug abuse prevention*. Juneau, AK: Department of Health and Social Services.

State Office of Drug Abuse. (1976). *Alaska state plan for drug abuse prevention*. Juneau, AK: Department of Health and Social Services.

State Office of Alcoholism and Drug Abuse. (1979). The Alaska state drugs abuse plan. Juneau, AK: The State Office of Alcoholism and Drug Abuse.

Tanner, L. (1987, Feb. 13). Smokeless tobacco use high among Native teen-agers. *Anchorage Daily News*, p. B-1.

Thompson, J. P., Emboden, W., & Fisher, D. G. (1985). Mushroom use by college students. *Journal of Drug Education, 15*(2), 111-124.

University of Michigan. (1989, Feb.). *Teen drug use continues to decline*. Ann Arbor, MI: The University of Michigan News and Information Service.

Westermeyer, J. (1987). Cultural patterns of drug and alcohol use: An analysis of host and agent in the cultural environment. *Bulletin on Narcotics, XXXIX*(2), 11-27.

World Health Organization. (1981). *Report of an ARF? WHO scientific meeting on adverse consequences of cannabis use*. Toronto: Addiction Research Foundation.

Zuckerman, M. (1983). *Biological bases of sensation seeking, impulsivity, and anxiety*. Hillsdale, NJ: Erlbaum.

Appendixes

APPENDIX 1. Student Survey: Anchorage, Barrow, Bethel, Cordova, Fairbanks, Juneau, Kotzebue

The Center for Alcohol and Addiction Studies

University of Alaska Anchorage

Confidential Student Questionnaire

Dear Student:

The purpose of this study is to help us to understand better your feelings and experiences with respect to alcohol and other drugs. In this survey use of drugs does not include prescription drugs or alcohol used in religious activities.

About 3,000 students across Alaska will take part in this study. Your answers will be kept absolutely confidential. There is no way to identify any student who responds. We do not ask your name - do not write it anywhere on the questionnaire. Your participation is voluntary. We need your help, and hope that you will contribute to the success of this study.

Thank you for your cooperation.

Directions

This is not a test, there are no right or wrong answers, and you are not timed on any section or group of questions. Please read all the directions for each question carefully, and follow the instructions for each item. It is important that you follow the order of questions within each section. If you do not understand or cannot read a question, raise your hand and someone will assist you.

When you have finished the questionnaire put it in the envelope that has been provided by the monitor. No one at the school will see or read your answers. The envelope will be sealed after the last questionnaire is completed. All the envelopes will be immediately taken to the University to be coded and entered into the computer. All questionnaires will be destroyed after the computer file has been set up.

Part 1. Background Information

1. I am

    _____ Female.
    _____ Male.

2. My ethnic background is: (Please check the correct one.)

    _____ Alaska Native   _____ Spanish (Hispanic)
    _____ American Indian   _____ White
    _____ Asian or Pacific Islander _____ Filipino
    _____ Black   _____ Other: Which? _____

3. How old were you as of your last birthday?   _____

4. What grade are you in? (Please check the correct one.)

    _____6th _____7th _____8th _____9th _____10th _____11th _____12th

5. Have you ever taken part in an alcohol or drug education/prevention program in one of your classes?

    _____ No (Go to #7.)
    _____ Yes (continue.)

6. Which grade(s) did you take part in an alcohol or drug education/prevention program?

    (Check all that apply.)

    _____ 5th grade or below   _____ 9th grade
    _____ 6th grade   _____ 10th grade
    _____ 7th grade   _____ 11th grade
    _____ 8th grade   _____ 12th grade

7. What grades do you usually get? (Check only the one that applies to you in each of the two columns.)

<u>During this school year</u>	<u>During the year before</u>
_____ Mostly A's	_____ Mostly A's
_____ Mostly A's and B's	_____ Mostly A's and B's
_____ Mostly B's	_____ Mostly B's
_____ Mostly B's and C's	_____ Mostly B's and C's
_____ Mostly C's	_____ Mostly C's
_____ Mostly C's and D's	_____ Mostly C's and D's
_____ Mostly D's and F's	_____ Mostly D's and F's

8. How many years have you lived in the municipality of Anchorage? (If you lived here, moved away, and returned, just count the most recent time.)   _____

Part 2. What follows is a set of questions asking about your experiences with different kinds of mood altering drugs used to get high or to feel good. Do not report the use of drugs used under the direction of a physician or dentist. Please respond to each of the following sections.

<u>**Section 1. Marijuana**</u>

Marijuana, which is sometimes called "grass," "pot," "weed," "smoke," "bud," "Mary Jane,"or "joint," is a substance that is usually smoked.

9. Have you ever had a chance to try marijuana? _____ No _____ Yes

10. Did you ever try marijuana?

_____ No (Go to **Section 2**.)
_____ Yes (Continue.)

11. How old were you when you first tried it? _____

12. Have you <u>ever</u> been high or stoned on marijuana to the point where you were pretty sure that you had experienced its effect?

_____ I never got high. _____ I have gotten high more than once.
_____ I have gotten high once. _____ I get high almost every time I use it.

13. How many different times have you used marijuana?

	No times	1-2 times	3-5 times	6-9 times	10-19 times	20-39 times	40+ times
Total times in your lifetime	___	___	___	___	___	___	___
Use during the last 12 months	___	___	___	___	___	___	___
Use during the last 30 days	___	___	___	___	___	___	___

Section 2. Cocaine.
Cocaine, which is called "coke," "toot," "blow," or "snow," or other names, is a white powdery substance that is usually sniffed or smoked.

14. Have you ever had a chance to try cocaine? _____ No _____ Yes

15. Did you ever try cocaine?

_____ No (Go to **Section 3**.)
_____ Yes (Continue.)

16. How did you use it? (Check all the apply to you.)

_____ I have sniffed it.
_____ I have smoked it.
_____ I have injected it (shot it up).
_____ I have used it in freebase form.

17. How old were you when you first tried it? _____

18. Have you ever been high on cocaine to the point where you were pretty sure that you had experienced its effect?

_____ I never got high. _____ I have gotten high more than once.
_____ I have gotten high once. _____ I get high almost every time I use it

19. How many different times have you used cocaine?

	No times	1-2 times	3-5 times	6-9 times	10-19 times	20-39 times	40+ times
Total times in your lifetime	___	___	___	___	___	___	___
Use during the last 12 months	___	___	___	___	___	___	___
Use during the last 30 days	___	___	___	___	___	___	___

Section 3. Crack

Another type of cocaine is called "crack." This form of cocaine looks like a piece of rock or soap, and is smoked.

20. Have you ever had a chance to try crack?   _____ No   _____ Yes

21. Did you ever try crack?

    _____ No (Go to **Section 4.**)
    _____ Yes (Continue.)

22. How old were you when you first tried it?_____

23. Have you ever been high on crack to the point where you were pretty sure that you had experienced its effect?

    _____ I never got high.
    _____ I have gotten high once.
    _____ I have gotten high more than once.
    _____ I get high almost every time I use it.

24. How many different times have you used crack?

	No times	1 - 2 times	3 - 5 times	6 - 9 times	10 - 19 times	20 - 39 times	40 + times
Total times in your lifetime	_____	_____	_____	_____	_____	_____	_____
Use during the last 12 months	_____	_____	_____	_____	_____	_____	_____
Use during the last 30 days	_____	_____	_____	_____	_____	_____	_____

Section 4. Stimulants ("Uppers")

Stimulants or amphetamine drugs, known as "uppers," "speed," "crystal," "bennies," "dexles," "pep pills," "crosstabs," "crossroads," and "crisscross," among other names, are used to make one feel more alert, energetic, or to obtain a high. They are usually taken in pill form.

25. Have you ever had a chance to try stimulants?   _____ No   _____ Yes

26. Did you ever try stimulants?

    _____ No (Go to **Section 5.**)
    _____ Yes (Continue.)

27. How old were you when you first tried any?   _____

28. Have you ever been high on a stimulant to the point where you were pretty sure that you had experienced its effect?

    _____ I never got high.
    _____ I have gotten high once.
    _____ I have gotten high more than once.
    _____ I get high almost every time I use it.

29. How many different times have you used stimulants?

	No times	1 - 2 times	3 - 5 times	6 - 9 times	10 - 19 times	20 - 39 times	40 + times
Total times in your lifetime	_____	_____	_____	_____	_____	_____	_____
Use during the last 12 months	_____	_____	_____	_____	_____	_____	_____
Use during the last 30 days	_____	_____	_____	_____	_____	_____	_____

Section 5. Hallucinogens

Hallucinogens, which are also called psychedelics, consist of such substances as LSD ("Acid"), Mescaline, and PCP, among other substances. Some of the slang names for hallucinogens are "mushrooms," "ecstasy," or "angel dust, " "window pane," and "blotter acid." These substances are used to experience hallucinations, or to alter how things are seen, change one's mood, feelings, or level of awareness.

30.   Have you ever had a chance to try hallucinogens?   _____ No   _____ Yes

31.   Did you ever try hallucinogens?

     _____ No (Go to **Section 6.**)
     _____ Yes (Continue.)

32.   How old were you when you first tried any?   _____

33.   Have you ever been high on an hallucinogen to the point where you were pretty sure that you had experienced its effect?

     _____ I never got high.
     _____ I have gotten high once
     _____ I have gotten high more than once.
     _____ I get high almost every time I use it.

34.   How many different times have you used hallucinogens?

	No times	1 - 2 times	3 - 5 times	6 - 9 times	10 - 19 times	20 - 39 times	40 + times
Total times in your lifetime	___	___	___	___	___	___	___
Use during the last 12 months	___	___	___	___	___	___	___
Use during the last 30 days	___	___	___	___	___	___	___

Section 6. Depressants ("Downers")

Depressant or "downer" type drugs, known as barbiturates, one of which is called Quaalude, are chemical substances used to calm oneself down or to get a high, much like using alcohol. Such drugs are usually taken in pill form, and are called "barbs," "blues" or "blue devils," "yellow jackets," "purple hearts," "soapers," or "ludes."

35.   Have you ever had a chance to try depressants?   _____ No   _____ Yes

36.   Did you ever try depressants?

     _____ No (Go to **Section 7.**)
     _____ Yes (Continue.)

37.   How old were you when you first tried any?   _____

38.   Have you ever been high on a depressant to the point where you were pretty sure that you had experienced its effect?

     _____ I never got high.
     _____ I have gotten high once
     _____ I have gotten high more than once.
     _____ I get high almost every time I use it.

39.   How many different times have you used depressants?

	No times	1-2 times	3-5 times	6-9 times	10-19 times	20-39 times	40+ times
Total times in your lifetime	___	___	___	___	___	___	___
Use during the last 12 months	___	___	___	___	___	___	___
Use during the last 30 days	___	___	___	___	___	___	___

Section 7. Heroin

Heroin, which is sometimes called "H," "horse," "junk," "Mexican brown," or "smack," can be a white or brownish powdery substance that can be injected (shot up), sniffed, or smoked.

40.   Have you ever had a chance to try heroin? ___ No   ___ Yes

41.   Did you ever try heroin?

___No (Go to **Section 8.**)
___Yes (Continue.)

42.   How old were you when you first tried it?   _____

43.   Have you ever been high on heroin to the point where you were pretty sure that you had experienced its effect?

_____ I never got high.
_____ I have gotten high once.
_____ I have gotten high more than once.
_____ I get high almost every time I use it.

44.   How many different times have you used heroin?

	No times	1-2 times	3-5 times	6-9 times	10-19 times	20-39 times	40+ times
Total times in your lifetime	___	___	___	___	___	___	___
Use during the last 12 months	___	___	___	___	___	___	___
Use during the last 30 days	___	___	___	___	___	___	___

Section 8. Inhalants

Inhalants are chemical substances, such as gasoline, kerosene, aerosol sprays, paint, glue, and other chemicals, or drugs such as nitrous oxide or amyl nitrate, that are sniffed or inhaled to induce a high.

45.   Have you ever had a chance to try inhalants? ___ No   ___ Yes

46.   Did you ever try inhalants?

_____   No(Go to **Section 9.**)
_____   Yes(Continue.)

47.   How old were you when you first tried any?   _____

48. Have you ever been high on an inhalant to the point where you were pretty sure that you had experienced its effect?

_____ I never got high.
_____ I have gotten high once.
_____ I have gotten high more than once.
_____ I get high almost every time I use it.

49. How many different times have you used inhalants?

	No times	1-2 times	3-5 times	6-9 times	10-19 times	20-39 times	40+ times
Total times in your lifetime	___	___	___	___	___	___	___
Use during the last 12 months	___	___	___	___	___	___	___
Use during the last 30 days	___	___	___	___	___	___	___

Section 9. Tranquilizers

Tranquilizers are substances used to calm oneself, to relax or to get high. One such drug is Valium.

50. Have you ever had a chance to try tranquilizers? _____ No _____ Yes

51. Did you ever try tranquilizers?

_____ No (Go to **Part 3.**)
_____ Yes (Continue.)

52. How old were you when you first tried any? _____

53. Have you ever been high on a tranquilizer to the point where you were pretty sure that you had experienced its effect?

_____ I never got high. _____ I have gotten high more than once.
_____ I have gotten high once. _____ I get high almost every time I use it.

54a. How many different times have you used tranquilizers?

	No times	1-2 times	3-5 times	6-9 times	10-19 times	20-39 times	40+ times
Total times in your lifetime	___	___	___	___	___	___	___
Use during the last 12 months	___	___	___	___	___	___	___
Use during the last 30 days	___	___	___	___	___	___	___

Part 3.

If you **HAVE NEVER TRIED A DRUG** answer #54b. If you have ever tried a drug, go to #55.

54b. If you have never tried a drug, was it because of any of the following reasons? (Check only one in each column that best applies to you for each item.)

Because of:	Very True of me	Often True of me	Sometimes True of me	Seldom True of me	Not True of me
Fear of damage to my mind	___	___	___	___	___
Moral reasons	___	___	___	___	___

Because of:	Very True of me	Often True of me	Sometimes True of me	Seldom True of me	Not True of me
Knowing friends who had a bad trip	___	___	___	___	___
Fear of having a bad experience	___	___	___	___	___
No opportunity to try a drug	___	___	___	___	___
Disappoint my parents	___	___	___	___	___
Pressure from friends	___	___	___	___	___
May cause addiction	___	___	___	___	___
It is illegal	___	___	___	___	___
Not important for me to try	___	___	___	___	___
Because of something I learned in school	___	___	___	___	___

(Go to #56.)

55. Have any of the following **ever happened to you** as a result of your experience with any type of drug? (Check all that apply to you.)

	Never	Once	2 - 3 times	4 or more times
Gotten into trouble with your teachers or principal.	___	___	___	___
Had it get in the way of school work	___	___	___	___
Gotten you in trouble with your friends	___	___	___	___
Gotten you in trouble with the police	___	___	___	___
Had a bad trip	___	___	___	___
Resulted in an accident or injury to you or others.	___	___	___	___
Been suspended from school	___	___	___	___
Been addicted	___	___	___	___

56. Do you think the use of any of the drugs listed below has **INCREASED** among students who attend your school during **the past year**? (Please check all the ones you believe have gone up.)

___ Alcohol	___ Cocaine	___ Stimulants
___ Tobacco	___ Crack	___ Depressants
___ Marijuana	___ Hallucinogens	___ Inhalants
___ Heroin	___ Tranquilizers	___ Don't know

57. Do you think the use of any of the drugs listed below has **DECREASED** among students who attend your school during **the past year**? (Please check all the ones you believe have gone down.)

___ Alcohol	___ Cocaine	___ Stimulants
___ Tobacco	___ Crack	___ Depressants
___ Marijuana	___ Hallucinogens	___ Inhalants
___ Heroin	___ Tranquilizers	___ Don't know

58. How many of your FRIENDS do you think **have tried:** (Check only one blank for each item.)

	None	1 or 2	Several	Most	All	Don't Know
Marijuana	___	___	___	___	___	___
Cocaine	___	___	___	___	___	___
Crack	___	___	___	___	___	___
Stimulants	___	___	___	___	___	___
Hallucinogens	___	___	___	___	___	___
Depressants	___	___	___	___	___	___
Heroin	___	___	___	___	___	___
Inhalants	___	___	___	___	___	___
Tranquilizers	___	___	___	___	___	___
Alcohol	___	___	___	___	___	___
Cigarettes	___	___	___	___	___	___
Smokeless tobacco	___	___	___	___	___	___

59. How many of your FRIENDS do you think **use**: (Check only one blank for each item.)

	None	1 or 2	Several	Most	All	Don't Know
Marijuana	___	___	___	___	___	___
Cocaine	___	___	___	___	___	___
Crack	___	___	___	___	___	___
Stimulants	___	___	___	___	___	___
Hallucinogens	___	___	___	___	___	___
Depressants	___	___	___	___	___	___
Heroin	___	___	___	___	___	___
Inhalants	___	___	___	___	___	___
Tranquilizers	___	___	___	___	___	___
Alcohol	___	___	___	___	___	___
Cigarettes	___	___	___	___	___	___
Smokeless tobacco	___	___	___	___	___	___

Part 4. The questions in this part ask about your experiences with other mood altering drugs such as beer, wine, and liquor.

60. Have you ever had a drink of wine, beer, or liquor - not just a sip or taste - with friends **outside** of your home?

_____ No (Go to **Part 5**.)
_____ Yes (Continue.)

61. Have you had a drink of wine, beer, or liquor - not just a sip or taste - with friends **outside** of your home **during the past year**?

_____ No
_____ Yes

62. How old were you when you had your **first** drink (not just a sip or taste) with friends at a party or some other kind of get together **outside** of your home? _____

63. During the **past 30 days**, how many times did you drink beer, wine, or liquor?
_____ None
_____ 1 time
_____ 2-3 times
_____ 1-2 times a week
_____ 3-4 times a week
_____ 5-6 times a week
_____ Once a day
_____ More than once a day

64. During **the past 30 days**, think of each time when you had beer, wine, or liquor. Each time you drink, how many drinks do you usually have? (Think of one can of beer, a glass of wine, or a mixed drink as equal to one drink.)

_____ I did not drink during this time
_____ 1 drink
_____ 2 drinks
_____ 3-5 drinks
_____ 6-10 drinks
_____ 11 or more drinks

65. During the **past year**, about how many times did you drink just to feel a little high or light-headed?

_____ None	_____ 2-3 times	_____ 6-10 times	_____ Twice a month
_____ One time	_____ 4-5 times	_____ Once a month	_____ Once a week or more

66. During the **past year**, about how many times have you gotten drunk or very, very high?

____ None ____ 2-3 times ____ 6-10 times ____ Twice a month
____ One time ____ 4-5 times ____ Once a month ____ Once a week or more

67. During the **past year**, about how many times have you gotten sick (nauseous or vomiting) as a result of drinking?

____ None ____ 2-3 times ____ 6-10 times ____ Twice a month
____ One time ____ 4-5 times ____ Once a month ____ Once a week or more

68. Have you **ever had** any of the following happen to you as a result of drinking? (Place a check where it applies to you for each item.)

	Never	Once	2-3 times	4 or more times
Gotten into trouble with your teachers or principal	___	___	___	___
Had it get in the way of school work	___	___	___	___
Gotten you in trouble with your friends	___	___	___	___
Gotten you in trouble with the police	___	___	___	___
Gotten you in a fight	___	___	___	___
Resulted in an accident or injury to you or others	___	___	___	___
Have driven when drinking	___	___	___	___

69. How many of your close friends drink alcoholic beverages at least once a week?

____ Most of my friends don't drink at all.
____ None of my friends drink at least once a week.
____ Some of my friends drink at least once a week.
____ Most of my friends drink at least once a week.
____ All of my friends drink at least once a week.

Part 5. Tobacco

70. Have you **ever** tried smoking cigarettes?

____ No (Go to #78.)
____ Yes (Continue.)

71. Have you smoked more than two or three times?

____ No
____ Yes

72. How old were you when you **first** tried smoking cigarettes? _____

73. During the **past 30 days**, how many times have you smoked cigarettes?

____ None (Go to #77)
____ 1 time
____ 2-3 times
____ 1-2 times a week
____ 3-4 times a week
____ 5-6 times a week
____ Once a day
____ Two or three times a day
____ More than four times a day

74. During **the past 30 days**, on the average, how many cigarettes have you smoked during a day?

_____ 1-5 cigarettes a day
_____ 6-10 cigarettes
_____ 11-15 cigarettes
_____ 16-20 cigarettes
_____ 21 or more cigarettes

75. Would you consider yourself:

_____ An occasional smoker (go to #79.)
_____ A light smoker (Go #76.)
_____ A moderate smoker (Go to #76.)
_____ A heavy smoker(Go to #76.)

76. How old were you when you became a light, moderate, or heavy smoker? _____

77. If you have stopped smoking, was it for any of these reasons? **IF YOU HAVE NOT QUIT, GO TO #79.** (Check all that apply to you.)

_____ Just didn't feel a need to smoke anymore
_____ Fear of damage to my body
_____ Parents disapproved
_____ Friends disapproved
_____ Because of something I learned in school
_____ Other:
    (Go to #79.)

78. If you have **never** smoked, was it for any of the following reasons? (Check all that apply to you.)

_____ Just didn't feel a need to smoke anymore
_____ Fear of damage to my body
_____ Parents disapproved
_____ Friends disapproved
_____ Because of something I learned in school
_____ Other:
    (Go to #79)

79. Have you **ever** tried chewing tobacco (such as Redman) or smokeless tobacco (such as Skoal)?

_____ No (Go to #86.)
_____ Yes

80. How old were you when you first tried chewing or smokeless tobacco? _____

81. How many times during the past month (30 days), have you used chewing tobacco?

_____ None
_____ 1 time
_____ 2-3 times
_____ 1-2 times a week
_____ 3-4 times a week
_____ 5-6 times a week
_____ Once a day
_____ Two or three times a day
_____ More than four times a day

82. How many times during the past month (30 days), have you used smokeless tobacco?

_____ None
_____ 1 time
_____ 2-3 times
_____ 1-2 times a week
_____ 3-4 times a week
_____ 5-6 times a week
_____ Once a day
_____ Two or three times a day
_____ More than four times a day

83. Would you consider yourself:

_____ An occasional user (Go to #85.)
_____ A moderate user (Go to #84.)
_____ A light user (Go to #84.)
_____ A heavy user (Go to #84.)

84. How old were you when you became a light, moderate, or heavy smokeless or chewing tobacco user? _____

85. If you have used smokeless or chewing tobacco but have now stopped, was it for any of these reasons? **IF YOU HAVE NOT QUIT SKIP TO PART 6.**
(Check all that apply to you.)

_____ Just didn't feel a need to use it anymore
_____ Fear of damage to my body
_____ Parents disapproved
_____ Friends disapproved
_____ Other: _____

86. If you have **never used** chewing or smokeless tobacco, was it for any of the following reasons? (Check all that apply to you.)

_____ Just don't feel a need to use it
_____ Friends disapproved
_____ Parents disapproved
_____ Fear of damage to my body
_____ Because of something I learned in school
_____ Other: _____

Part 6
Please answer the following questions **whether you have used drugs or not** concerning some different feelings or experiences that people have. Read each item and check the statement that best describes you. Answer every item.

Because of:	Very True of me	Often True of me	Sometimes True of me	Seldom True of me	Not True of me
I would enjoy being a famous person.					
I don't really have fun at parties.					
I often act without thinking.					
I enjoy being alone.					
I am pretty cautious.					
I daydream about doing hard tasks.					
I care what others think about me.					
I do not give up easily on a problem.					

Because of:	Very True of me	Often True of me	Sometimes True of me	Seldom True of me	Not True of me
I feel that I have a lot of control over my future	___	___	___	___	___
I often wish I had more good friends.	___	___	___	___	___
My daydreams often cheer me up when I feel sad.	___	___	___	___	___
I almost never ask for help or advice.	___	___	___	___	___
Being successful is important to me.	___	___	___	___	___
I like to tell others how to do things.	___	___	___	___	___
I try not to take life very seriously.	___	___	___	___	___
When I want something - I want it now - not later.	___	___	___	___	___
I'm afraid I'm not very popular.	___	___	___	___	___
I am not interested in anything unless it is exciting.	___	___	___	___	___
My feelings are easily hurt.	___	___	___	___	___
I sometimes question the reason why I do things.	___	___	___	___	___
Sometimes I take myself too seriously.	___	___	___	___	___
Being successful at what I do is important to me.	___	___	___	___	___
What others think of me is not important to me.	___	___	___	___	___
I like to feel free to come and go as I please.	___	___	___	___	___
I am not easily pressured by my friends.	___	___	___	___	___

This is the end of the questionnaire.

Thank you for help.

APPENDIX 2. Nome Questionnaire

The Center for Alcohol and Addiction Studies

University of Alaska, Anchorage

Confidential Student Questionnaire

Dear Student:

The purpose of this study is to help us to understand better your feelings and experiences with respect to alcohol and other drugs. About 3,000 students across Alaska will take part in this study. Your answers will be kept absolutely confidential. There is no way to identify any student who responds. We do not ask your name - do not write it anywhere on the questionnaire. Your participation is voluntary. We need your help, and hope that you will contribute to the success of this study.

Thank you for your cooperation.

Directions

This is not a test and you are not timed on any section or group of questions. Please read carefully all the directions for each question. It is important that you follow the order of questions within each section. If you do not understand or cannot read a question raise your hand and someone will assist you. When you have finished the questionnaire put it in the envelope that has been provided by the monitor. No one at the school will see or read your answers. The envelope will be sealed after the last questionnaire is completed. All the envelopes will be immediately taken to the University to be coded and entered into the computer. All questionnaires will be destroyed after the computer file has been set up.

Part 1. Background Information

1. I am
   ___Female
   ___Male

2. My ethnic background is? (Please check the correct one.)
   ___Alaska Native   ___Hispanic
   ___American Indian   ___White
   ___Asian or Pacific Islander   ___Other: Which_____
   ___Black

3. How old were you as of your last birthday?_____

4. What grade are you in? (Please check the correct one.)

   ___6th ___7th ___8th ___9th ___10th ___11th ___12th

5. Have you ever taken part in an alcohol or drug education/prevention program in one of your classes?
   ___No (Go to #7)
   ___Yes (continue)

6. Which grade(s) did you take part in a drug education program? (Check all that apply)
   ___5th grade or below   ___9th grade
   ___6th grade   ___10th grade
   ___7th grade   ___11th grade
   ___8th grade   ___12th grade

7. What grades do you usually get? (Check only the one that applies to you in each of the two columns.)

During this school year	During the year before
___Mostly A's	___Mostly A's
___Mostly A's and B's	___Mostly A's and B's
___Mostly B's	___Mostly B's
___Mostly B's and C's	___Mostly B's and C's
___Mostly C's	___Mostly C's
___Mostly C's and D's	___Mostly C's and D's
___Mostly D's and F's	___Mostly D's and F's

8. How many years have you lived in this community?_____

Part 2. This part asks about any experiences with drugs that you may have tried without a prescription.

9. Have you ever had any chance to try any of the drugs listed below? Check all that were possible.

___ Marijuana (pot, hash)   ___Depressants (downers)

___ Inhalants (Gasoline, Glue, etc.)   ___Tranquilizers (librium, valium, etc.)

___Hallucinogens (LSD, PCP)   ___Alcohol (beer, wine, liquor)

___Cocaine (coke)   ___Crack (rock)

___Tobacco (cigarettes)   ___Chewing Tobacco

___ Heroin (smack)   ___Stimulants (uppers)

10. If you have tried a drug, how many times have you ever used any of the ones listed below during your lifetime? Check the column that best describes your experience with each drug. If you have Never tried a drug skip to Part 3.

	Never Used	1-2 Times	3-5 Times	6-9 Times	10-19 Times	20-39 Times	40+ Times
Marijuana (pot, hash)							
Inhalants (gasoline, glue, etc.)							
Hallucinogens (LSD, PCP)							
Cocaine (coke)							
Crack							
Heroin (smack)							
Stimulants (uppers)							
Depressants (downers)							

11. How many times have you ever used any of the ones listed below during the past year? Check the column that best describes your experience with each drug.

	Never Used	1-2 Times	3-5 Times	6-9 Times	10-19 Times	20-39 Times	40+ Times
Marijuana (pot, hash)							
Inhalants (gasoline, glue, etc.)							
Hallucinogens (LSD, PCP)							
Cocaine (coke)							
Crack							
Heroin (smack)							
Stimulants (uppers)							
Depressants (downers)							

12. How many times have you ever used any of the ones listed below during the past 30 days?
Check the column that best describes your experience with each drug.

	Never Used	1-2 Times	3-5 Times	6-9 Times	10-19 Times	20-39 Times	40+ Times
Marijuana (pot, hash)							
Inhalants (gasoline, glue, etc.)							
Hallucinogens (LSD, PCP)							
Cocaine (coke)							
Crack							
Heroin (smack)							
Stimulants (uppers)							
Depressants (downers)							

13. If you have tried one of the substances listed above, please report the age you first tried it for every one that you tried.

Marijuana_____   Inhalants_____

Hallucinogens_____   Cocaine_____

Crack_____   Heroin_____

Stimulants_____   Depressants_____

Tranquilizers_____

Part 3.
If you HAVE NEVER TRIED A DRUG answer #14. If you have tried a drug, skip to #15.

14. If you have never tried a drug, was it because of any of the following?
   (Check only one in each column that best applies to you for each item.)

Because of:	Very True of me	Often True of me	Sometimes True for of me	Seldom True of me	Not True of me
Fear of damage to my mind	__	__	__	__	__
Moral reasons	__	__	__	__	__
Knowing friends who had a bad trip	__	__	__	__	__
Fear of having a bad experience	__	__	__	__	__
No opportunity to try a drug	__	__	__	__	__
Disappoint my parents	__	__	__	__	__
Pressure from friends	__	__	__	__	__
May cause addiction	__	__	__	__	__
It is illegal	__	__	__	__	__
Not important for me to try	__	__	__	__	__
Because of something I learned in school.	__	__	__	__	__

(Skip to # 16)

15. Have any of the following ever happened to you as a result of your experience with any type of drug? (Check all that apply to you.)

	Never	Once	2-3 Times	4 or more Times
Gotten into trouble with your teachers or principal...	__	__	__	__
Had it get in the way of school work...............	__	__	__	__
Gotten you in trouble with your friends............	__	__	__	__
Gotten you in trouble with the police..............	__	__	__	__
Had a bad trip..............................	__	__	__	__
Resulted in an accident or injury to you or others....	__	__	__	__
Been suspended from school...................	__	__	__	__

(Continue with #16)

16. Do you think the use of any of the drugs listed below has **INCREASED** in your school during the past year? (Please check all the ones you believe have gone up.)

___Alcohol   ___Cocaine   ___Stimulants
___Tobacco   ___Crack   ___Depressants
___Marijuana   ___Hallucinogens   ___Inhalants
___Heroin   ___Tranquilizers

17. Do you think the use of any of the drugs listed below has **DECREASED** in your school during the past year? (Please check all the ones you believe have gone down.)

___Alcohol   ___Cocaine   ___Stimulants
___Tobacco   ___Crack   ___Depressants
___Marijuana   ___Hallucinogens   ___Inhalants
___Heroin   ___Tranquilizers

18. How many of your FRIENDS do you think have tried: (Check only one blank for each item.)

	None	1 or 2	Several	Most	All	Don't Know
Marijuana............	__	__	__	__	__	__
Cocaine.............	__	__	__	__	__	__
Crack..............	__	__	__	__	__	__
Stimulants...........	__	__	__	__	__	__
Hallucinogens........	__	__	__	__	__	__
Depressants.........	__	__	__	__	__	__
Heroin.............	__	__	__	__	__	__
Inhalants............	__	__	__	__	__	__
Tranquilizers.........	__	__	__	__	__	__
Alcohol.............	__	__	__	__	__	__
Cigarettes...........	__	__	__	__	__	__
Smokeless tobacco....	__	__	__	__	__	__

19. How many of your FRIENDS do you think use: (Check only one blank for each item.)

	None	1 or 2	Several	Most	All	Don't Know
Marijuana............	__	__	__	__	__	__
Cocaine.............	__	__	__	__	__	__
Crack..............	__	__	__	__	__	__
Stimulants...........	__	__	__	__	__	__
Hallucinogens........	__	__	__	__	__	__
Depressants.........	__	__	__	__	__	__
Heroin.............	__	__	__	__	__	__
Inhalants............	__	__	__	__	__	__
Alcohol.............	__	__	__	__	__	__
Cigarettes...........	__	__	__	__	__	__
Smokeless tobacco....	__	__	__	__	__	__

Part 4. The questions in this part ask about your experiences with beer, wine, and liquor.

20. Have you ever had a drink of wine, beer, or liquor - not just a sip or taste - with friends outside of   your home?

>   ___No (Go to Part 5)
>   ___Yes (Continue)

21. Have you had a drink of wine, beer, or liquor - not just a sip or taste - with friends outside of your home **during the past year?**

>   ___No
>   ___Yes

22. How old were you when you had your **first** drink (not just a sip or taste) with friends at a party or some other kind of get together **outside** of your home? _____

23. During the **past 30 days**, how many times did you drink beer, wine, or liquor?
>   ___No time
>   ___1 time
>   ___2-3 times
>   ___1-2 times a week
>   ___3-4 times a week
>   ___5-6 times a week
>   ___Once a day
>   ___More than once a day

24. During **the past 30 days**, think of each time when you had beer, wine, or liquor. Each time you drink, how many drinks do you usually have?
(Think of one can of beer, a glass of wine, or a mixed drink as equal to one drink.)
>   ___I did not drink during this time
>   ___1 drink
>   ___2 drinks
>   ___3-5 drinks
>   ___6-10 drinks
>   ___11 or more drinks

25. During the **past year**, about how many times did you drink just to feel a little high or light-headed?

| ___None | ___2-3 times | ___6-10 times | ___Twice a month |
| ___One time | ___4-5 times | ___Once a month | ___Once a week or more |

26. During the **past year**, about how many times have you gotten drunk or very, very high?

| ___None | ___2-3 times | ___6-10 times | ___Twice a month |
| ___One time | ___4-5 times | ___Once a month | ___Once a week or more |

27. During the **past year**, about how many times have you gotten sick (nauseous or vomiting) as a result of drinking?

| ___None | ___2-3 times | ___6-10 times | ___Twice a month |
| ___One time | ___4-5 times | ___Once a month | ___Once a week or more |

28. Have you **ever had** any of the following happen to you as a result of drinking?
>   (Place a check where it applies to you for each item.)

Times	Never	Once	2-3 Times	4 or more
Gotten into trouble with your teachers or principal. .	—	—	—	—
Had it get in the way of school work.	—	—	—	—
Gotten you in trouble with your friends.	—	—	—	—
Gotten you in trouble with the police.	—	—	—	—
Gotten you in a fight.	—	—	—	—
Resulted in an accident or injury to you or others. . . .	—	—	—	—
Have driven when drinking?.	—	—	—	—

29. How many of your close friends drink alcoholic beverages at least once a week?
___Most of my friends don't drink at all
___None of my friends drink at least once a week
___Some of my friends drink at least once a week
___Most of my friends drink at least once a week
___All of my friends drink at least once a week

Part 5. Tobacco
30. Have you ever tried smoking cigarettes?
___No (Go to #38)
___Yes (Continue)

31. Have you smoked more than two or three times and then stopped?
___No (Continue)
___Yes (Go to # 38)

32. How old were you when you first tried smoking cigarettes?_____

33. During the past 30 days, how many times have you smoked cigarettes?
___None (Go to #37)
___1 time
___2-3 times
___1-2 times a week
___3-4 times a week
___5-6 times a week
___Once a day
___Two or three times a day
___More than four times a day

34. During the past 30 days, on the average, how many cigarettes have you smoked during a day?

___1-5 cigarettes a day
___6-10 cigarettes
___11-15 cigarettes
___16-20 cigarettes
___21 or more cigarettes

35. Would you consider yourself:
___An occasional smoker (go to #39)   ___A moderate smoker (Go to #36)
___A light smoker (Go #36)   ___A heavy smoker(Go to #36)

36. How old were you when you became a light, moderate, or heavy smoker?_____

37. If you have stopped smoking, was it for any of these reasons? IF YOU HAVE NOT QUIT GO TO #39.   (Check all that apply to you.)

___Just didn't feel a need to smoke anymore
___Fear of damage to my body
___Parents disapproved
___Friends disapproved
___Because of something I learned in school
___Other:_____
(Go to #39)

38. If you have never smoked, was it for any of the following reasons? (Check all that apply to you.)
___Just don't feel a need to smoke
___Fear of damage to my body
___Parents disapproved
___Friends disapproved
___Because of something I learned in school
___Other:_____
(Go to #39)

39. Have you <u>ever</u> tried chewing tobacco or smokeless tobacco (such as Skoal)?

    ___No (Go to #45)

    ___Yes

40. How old were you when you first tried chewing or smokeless tobacco?_____

41. How many times during the past month (30 days) have you used chewing tobacco?

    ___None
    ___1 time
    ___2-3 times
    ___1-2 times a week.
    ___3-4 times a week
    ___5-6 times a week.
    ___Once a day
    ___More than once a day

41. How many times during the past month (30 days) have you used smokeless tobacco?

    ___None
    ___1 time
    ___2-3 times
    ___1-2 times a week.
    ___3-4 times a week
    ___5-6 times a week.
    ___Once a day
    ___More than once a day

42. Would you consider yourself:

    ___An occasional user   ___A light user
    ___A moderate user   ___A heavy user

43. How old were you when you became a light, moderate, or heavy smokeless or chewing tobacco user?_____

44. If you have used smokeless or chewing tobacco but have now stopped, was it for any of these reasons? **IF YOU HAVE NOT QUIT SKIP TO PART 6.** (Check all that apply to you.)

    ___Just didn't feel a need to use it anymore   ___Fear of damage to my body
    ___Parents disapproved   ___Friends disapproved
    ___Other:_____

45. If you have <u>never used</u> chewing or smokeless tobacco, was it for any of the following reasons?   (Check all that apply to you.)

    ___Just don't feel a need to use it
    ___Friends disapproved
    ___Parents disapproved
    ___Fear of damage to my body
    ___Because of something I learned in school
    ___Other:_____

PLEASE GO TO PART 6 ON THE NEXT PAGE

Part 6

Please answer the following questions, whether you have used drugs or not, concerning some different feelings or experiences that people have. Read each item and check the statement that best describes you. Answer every item.

	Very True of me	Often True of me	Sometimes True of me	Seldom True of me	Not True of me
I would enjoy being a famous person.........	—	—	—	—	—
I don't really have fun at parties...........	—	—	—	—	—
I often act without thinking...............	—	—	—	—	—
I enjoy being alone.....................	—	—	—	—	—
I am pretty cautious.....................	—	—	—	—	—
I daydream about doing hard tasks...........	—	—	—	—	—
I care what others think about me...........	—	—	—	—	—
I do not give up easily on a problem..........	—	—	—	—	—
I feel that I have a lot of control over my future.	—	—	—	—	—
I often wish I had more good friends.........	—	—	—	—	—
My daydreams often cheer me up when I feel sad...............................	—	—	—	—	—
I almost never ask for help or advice.........	—	—	—	—	—
Being successful is important to me..........	—	—	—	—	—
I like to tell others how to do things..........	—	—	—	—	—
I try not to take life very seriously...........	—	—	—	—	—
When I want something - I want it now - not later...............................	—	—	—	—	—
I'm afraid I'm not very popular..............	—	—	—	—	—
I am not interested in anything unless it is exciting...............................	—	—	—	—	—
My feelings are easily hurt.................	—	—	—	—	—
I sometimes question the reason why I do things.................................	—	—	—	—	—
Sometimes I take myself too seriously......	—	—	—	—	—
Being successful at what I do is important to me..................................	—	—	—	—	—
What others think of me is not important to me.	—	—	—	—	—
I like to feel free to come and go as I please ...	—	—	—	—	—
I am not easily pressured by my friends......	—	—	—	—	—

This is the end of the questionnaire

Thank you for help

APPENDIX 3. Sitka Questionnaire

CONFIDENTIAL

This questionnaire is part of a study being conducted to help us better understand the feelings and experiences of students as they relate to drugs.

Your participation is <u>voluntary</u> and you do not have to answer the questions unless you want to. However, we need your help and would like you to answer all of the questions.

If you don't understand or can't read a question, raise your hand and someone will help you.

This survey is strictly confidential. No one can know what you put down except you. <u>Do not put your name anywhere on the questionnaire.</u>

Thank you for your help.

Part I

1. During the last school year, did you have any drug/alcohol education lessons as part of any class? (Circle one number)

   1. No   2. Yes   3. Don't Know

2. Do you believe that there is a need for drug/alcohol education programs in your school? (Circle one number)

   1. No   2. Yes   3. Don't Know

Now we would like to ask you about alcohol products.

3. Have you ever drank wine, beer or some other alcoholic beverage on your own -- not just having a taste of someone else's drink?

   1. No   2. Yes

          A. If yes, do you drink alcoholic beverages now?

          1. No   2. Yes

          If yes, how often?

          0. A few times a year

          1. About once a month or less

          2. About 2 or 3 times a month

          3. About once a week

          4. About 2-5 times a week

          5. About once a day

          6. More than once a day

SKIP TO
QUESTION 4   B. How many different times have you used alcohol in the past year?

          1. Never

          2. 1-2 times

          3. 3-5 times

          4. 6-9 times

          5. 10-19 times

          6. 20-39 times

          7. 40+ times

C. How old were you when you first tried it? _____

D. When was the last time you tried it?

_____ More than a year ago

_____ Months ago

_____ Weeks ago

_____ This week

E. The following questions are about some things which may not have happened to you. Please circle whether each statement is true or false for you.

I have missed school because of alcohol use.   T   F

I have had problems in school because of
alcohol use.   T   F

My grades have been affected because of the
use of alcohol.   T   F

I have had problems outside of school
because of alcohol use.   T   F

I have never had any kind of problem
at school because of alcohol use.   T   F

4. If you have <u>never tried or have stopped</u> using alcoholic beverages, was it for any of the following reasons? Please circle either yes or no for each item.

1. May hurt by body.   5. Friends disapprove.

    1. No   2. Yes   1. No   2. Yes

2. May hurt my mind.   6. Not important for me to try it.

    1. No   2. Yes   1. No   2. Yes

3. May cause addiction.   7. Never had the chance.

    1. No   2. Yes   1. No   2. Yes

4. It is illegal.   8. May affect my participation in sports.

    1. No   2. Yes   1. No   2. Yes

                                   9. Other: _____

                                       _____

5. If you wanted to try using a drug other than <u>alcohol</u> or <u>tobacco</u>, how easy or difficult would it be for you to get it? (Circle one number)

1. Impossible

2. Difficult

3. Fairly easy

4. Very easy

Now we would like to ask you about some drugs that are usually used for non-medical reasons, such as marijuana.

6. Marijuana is sometimes called grass or pot, and hashish is sometimes referred to as hash. Have you ever been offered this drug?

   1. No   2. Yes_____

   If yes, did you try it?

   1. No   2. Yes

   If yes, how old were you when you first tried it?

   _____

   When was the last time you tried it?

   _____ more than a year ago?

   _____ months ago

   _____ weeks ago

7. How about psychedelics like LSD, mescaline, psilocybin, MDA, or STP and that sort of thing? Have you ever been offered any of these drugs?

   1. No   2. Yes_____

   If yes, did you try it?

   1. No   2. Yes

   If yes, how old were you when you first tried it?

   _____

   When was the last time you tried it?

   _____ more than a year ago?

   _____ months ago

   _____ weeks ago

8. Have you ever been offered cocaine (or crack)?

   1. No   2. Yes_____

   If yes, did you try it?

   1. No   2. Yes

   If yes, how old were you when you first tried it?

   _____

   When was the last time you tried it?

   _____ more than a year ago?

   _____ months ago
   _____ weeks ago

9. Have you ever been offered   If yes, did you try it?
   heroin (or smack) ?
                                 1. No   2. Yes

                                 If yes, how old
                                 were you when you
   1. No   2. Yes_____ first tried it?

                                 _____

                                 When was the last
                                 time you tried it?

                                        more than a
                                 _____ year ago?
                                 _____ months ago
                                 _____ weeks ago

10. Have you ever been offered an   If yes, did you try it?
    inhalant - by that we mean drugs
    and other substances people sniff 1. No   2. Yes
    or inhale for the effect - things
    like glue, aerosol sprays, ether, If yes, how old
    gasoline, or that sort of thing?   were you when you
                                       first tried it?
    1. No   2. Yes_____

                                       _____

                                       When was the last
                                       time you tried it?

                                              more than a
                                       _____ year ago?
                                       _____ months ago
                                       _____ weeks ago

Now we would like to ask about some drugs which <u>can be</u> prescribed by doctors.
However, we're <u>only interested</u> in times you used these drugs to get high, or
just to feel good, or for other <u>non-medical</u> purposes. That is, when they were
not given to you by a doctor.

11. Amphetamines and other stimulants   If yes, did you try it?
    are sometimes called speed or uppers.
    People can take them to lose weight,   1. No   2. Yes
    stay awake, or feel more energetic.
    Have you ever been offered this   If yes, how old
    type of drug?   were you when you
                                            first tried it?
    1. No   2. Yes_____

                                            _____

                                            When was the last
                                            time you tried it?

                                                   more than a
                                            _____ year ago?
                                            _____ months ago
                                            _____ weeks ago

12. How about sleeping pills, barbiturates and other sedatives which can be taken to help people sleep or calm down? People also use these to get high or for other non-medical purposes.

    1. No   2. Yes_____

    If yes, did you try it?

    1. No   2. Yes

    If yes, how old were you when you first tried it?

    _____

    When was the last time you tried it?

    _____ more than a year ago?
    _____ months ago
    _____ weeks ago

13. How about tranquilizers and other downers which can be taken to help people relax?

    1. No   2. Yes_____

    If yes, did you try it?

    1. No   2. Yes

    If yes, how old were you when you first tried it?

    _____

    When was the last time you tried it?

    _____ more than a year ago?
    _____ months ago
    _____ weeks ago

14. If you have used any of the chemicals listed below, mark and X in the box that indicates how many different times you used it during the past year.

	Not at all	About once a month or less	About 2 or 3 times a month	About once a week	About 2-5 times a week	About once a day	More than once a day
1. Marijuana (pot)							
2. Psychedelics (LSD, PCP)							
3. Cocaine (coke)							
4. Heroin (smack)							
5. Inhalants (gasoline, glue)							
6. Stimulants (uppers)							

	Not at all	About once a month or less	About 2 or 3 times a month	About once a week	About 2-5 times a week	About once a day	More than once a day
7. Sedatives (downers)							
8. Tranquilizers (Valium, etc.)							

*NOW, IT YOU HAVE EVER USED ANY OF THE ABOVE DRUGS, PLEASE GO BACK AND CIRCLE THE FIRST ONE YOU EVER USED.

15. The following questions are about some things which may have or may not have happened to you. Please circle whether each statement is true or false for you.

I have missed school because of drug use.　　　T　　F

I have had problems in school because of drug use.　　　T　　F

My grades have been affected because of the use of drugs.　　　T　　F

I have had problems outside of school because of drug use.　　　T　　F

I have never had any kind of problem at school because of drug use.　　　T　　F

16. If you have never tried or have stopped using marijuana, cocaine, or other chemicals, was it for any of the following reasons? Please circle either yes or not for each item.

1. May hurt by body.　　　　　　5. Friends disapprove.

　　1. No　2. Yes　　　　　　　　1. No　2. Yes

2. May hurt my mind.　　　　　　6. Not important for me to try it.

　　1. No　2. Yes　　　　　　　　1. No　2. Yes

3. May cause addiction.　　　　　7. Never had the chance.

　　1. No　2. Yes　　　　　　　　1. No　2. Yes

4. It is illegal.　　　　　　　　8. Other: _____

　　1. No　2. Yes　　　　　　　　_____

17. Now, we would like to ask a few general questions about you.

1. Your sex (please circle one number)　　　2. Age to nearest birthday?

　　1. Female　2. Male

　　　　　　　　　　　　　　　　　　　　　　_____

3. Circle your grade in school.

   Junior High   High School

       6   7   8   9   10   11   12

THIS IS THE END OF THE QUESTIONNAIRE

THANK YOU FOR FILLING IT OUT